LifeLight

"In Him was life, and that life was the light of men." John 1:4

John, Part 1

—

JOHN 1–11

LEADERS GUIDE

CPH®
SAINT LOUIS

Earl H. Gaulke, editor

Revised from material prepared by Milton Rudnick and Roger Sonnenberg

This publication is available in braille and in large print for the visually impaired. Write to the Library for the Blind, 1333 S. Kirkwood Road, St. Louis, MO 63122-7295; or call 1-800-433-3954.

Cover painting: Apparition of Christ at the Lake of Tiberiade/SuperStock/Peter Willi

1   2   3   4   5   6   7   8   9   10   10   09   08   07   06   05   04   03   02   01

Contents

Introducing the LifeLight Program   5

Session 1—Lecture Leader   The Messenger Is the Message   9
                                John 1:1–18

Session 2—Lecture Leader   Introducing the Messenger   15
                                John 1:19–2:25

Session 3—Lecture Leader   One-on-One   21
                                John 3:1–4:42

Session 4—Lecture Leader   Communication through Healing   27
                                John 4:43–5:47

Session 5—Lecture Leader   Life-Giving Communication   33
                                John 6:1–71

Session 6—Lecture Leader   Communication Breakdown   39
                                John 7:1–8:30

Session 7—Lecture Leader   Communication Breakthrough   45
                                John 8:31–9:41

Session 8—Lecture Leader   Communication at Its Best   51
                                John 10:1–42

Session 9—Lecture Leader   Ultimate Purpose: Death-Transcending Relationships   55
                                John 11:1–57

Session 1—Small-Group Leader   The Messenger Is the Message   61
                                John 1:1–18

Session 2—Small-Group Leader   Introducing the Messenger   65
                                John 1:19–2:25

Session 3—Small-Group Leader   One-on-One   69
                                John 3:1–4:42

Session 4—Small-Group Leader   Communication through Healing   73
                                John 4:43–5:47

Session 5—Small-Group Leader   Life-Giving Communication   76
                                John 6:1–71

Session 6—Small-Group Leader   Communication Breakdown   79
                                John 7:1–8:30

Session 7—Small-Group Leader   Communication Breakthrough   82
                                John 8:31–9:41

Session 8—Small-Group Leader   Communication at Its Best   85
                                John 10:1–42

Session 9—Small-Group Leader   Ultimate Purpose: Death-Transcending Relationships   88
                                John 11:1–57

Appendix: Blacklines for Lecture 1   91

Introduction

Welcome to LifeLight

A special pleasure is in store for you. You will be instrumental in leading your brothers and sisters in Christ closer to Him who is our life and light (John 1:4). You will have the pleasure of seeing fellow Christians discover new insights and rediscover old ones as they open the Scriptures and dig deep into them, perhaps deeper than they have ever dug before. More than that, you will have the pleasure of sharing in this wonderful study.

LifeLight—An In-depth Study

LifeLight is a series of in-depth Bible studies. The goal of LifeLight is that through a regular program of in-depth personal and group study of Scripture, more and more Christian adults may grow in their personal faith in Jesus Christ, enjoy fellowship with the members of His body, and reach out in love to others in witness and service.

In-depth means that this Bible study includes the following four components: individual daily home study; discussion in a small group; a lecture presentation on the Scripture portion under study; and an enhancement of the week's material (through reading the enrichment magazine).

LifeLight Participants

LifeLight participants are adults who desire a deeper study of the Scriptures than is available in the typical Sunday morning adult Bible class. (Mid-to-older teens might also be LifeLight participants.) While LifeLight does not assume an existing knowledge of the Bible or special experience or skills in Bible study, it does assume a level of commitment that will bring participants to each of the nine weekly assemblies having read the assigned readings and attempted to answer the study questions. Daily reading and study will require from 15 to 30 minutes for the five days preceding the LifeLight assembly. The day following the assembly will be spent reviewing the previous week's study by going over the completed study leaflet and the enrichment magazine.

LifeLight Leadership

While the in-depth process used by LifeLight begins with individual study and cannot achieve its aims without this individual effort, it cannot be completed by individual study alone. Therefore, trained leaders are necessary. You fill one or perhaps more of the important roles described below.

The Director

This person oversees the LifeLight program in a local center (which may be a congregation or a center operated by several neighboring congregations). The director

- serves as the parish LifeLight overall coordinator and leader;
- coordinates the scheduling of the LifeLight program;
- orders materials;
- convenes LifeLight leadership team meetings;
- develops publicity materials;
- recruits participants;
- maintains records and budgeting;
- assigns, with the leadership team, participants to small discussion groups;
- makes arrangements for facilities;
- communicates outreach opportunities to small-group leaders and to congregational boards;
- follows up on participants who leave the program.

The Assistant Director *(optional)*

This person may assist the director. Duties listed for the director may be assigned to the assistant director as mutually agreeable.

The Lecture Leader

This person prepares and delivers the lecture at the weekly assembly. **(Lesson material for the lecture leader begins on p. 9.)** The lecture leader

- prepares and presents the Bible study lecture to the large group;

- prepares worship activities (devotional thought, hymn, prayer), using resources in the study leaflet and leaders guide and possibly other, outside sources;

- helps the small-group discussion leaders to grow in understanding the content of the lessons;

- encourages prayer at weekly leadership team and discussion leaders meetings.

The Small-Group Coordinator *(optional; the director may fill this role)*

This person supervises and coordinates the work of the small-group discussion leaders. The small-group coordinator

- recruits with the leadership team the small-group discussion leaders;

- trains or arranges for training of the discussion leaders;

- assists the director and discussion leaders in follow-up and outreach;

- encourages the discussion leaders to contact absent group members;

- participates in the weekly leadership team and discussion leaders equipping meetings;

- provides ongoing training and support as needed.

The Small-Group Discussion Leaders

These people guide and facilitate discussion of LifeLight participants in the small groups. **(Lesson material for the small-group leaders begins on p. 59.)** There should be one discussion leader for every group of no more than 12 participants. The small-group discussion leaders are, perhaps, those individuals who are most important to the success of the program. They should, therefore, be chosen with special care and be equipped with skills needed to guide discussion and to foster a caring fellowship within the group. These discussion leaders

- prepare each week for the small-group discussion by using the study leaflet and small-group leaders guide section for that session **(see p. 61)**;

- read the enrichment magazine as a study supplement;

- guide and facilitate discussion in their small group;

- encourage and assist the discussion group in prayer;

- foster fellowship and mutual care within the discussion group;

- attend weekly discussion leaders training meetings.

Leadership Training

LifeLight leaders will meet weekly to review the previous week's work and plan the coming week. At this session, leaders can address concerns and prepare for the coming session. LifeLight is a $1^{1}/_{2}$-hour program with no possibility for it to be taught in the one hour typically available on Sunday mornings. Some congregations, however, may want to use the Sunday morning Bible study hour for LifeLight preparation and leadership training. In such a meeting, the lecture leader and/or small-group coordinator may lead the discussion leaders through the coming week's lesson, reserving 5 or 10 minutes for problem solving or other group concerns.

While it requires intense effort, LifeLight has proven to bring great benefit to LifeLight participants. The effort put into this program, both by leaders and by participants, will be rewarding and profitable.

The LifeLight Weekly Schedule

Here is how LifeLight will work week by week:

1. Before session 1, each participant will receive the study leaflet for session 1 and the enrichment magazine for the course. The study leaflet contains worship resources (for use both in individual daily study and at the opening of the following week's assembly) and readings and study questions for five days. Challenge questions will lead those participants who have the time and desire a greater challenge into even deeper levels of study.

2. After the five days of individual study at home, participants will gather for a weekly assembly of all LifeLight participants. The assembly will begin with a brief period of worship (5 minutes). Participants will then join their assigned small discussion groups (of 12 or fewer, who will remain the same throughout the course), where they will go over the week's study questions together (55 minutes). Assembling together once again, participants will listen to a lecture presentation on the readings they have studied in the previous week and discussed in their small

groups (20 minutes). After the lecture presentation, the director or another leader will distribute the study leaflet for the following week. Closing announcements and other necessary business may take another five minutes before dismissal.

In some places some small groups will not join the weekly assembly because of scheduling or other reasons. Such groups may meet at another time and place (perhaps in the home of one of the small group's members). They will follow the same schedule, but they may use a cassette tape to listen to the week's lecture presentation. The discussion leader will obtain the tape and leaflets from the director. A cassette tape version of the lecture is available for purchase from CPH (see your catalogue). Or a congregation may record the lecture given by the lecture leader at the weekly assembly and duplicate it for use by other groups meeting later in the week.

3. On the day following the assembly, participants will review the preceding week's work by rereading the study leaflet they completed (and that they perhaps supplemented or corrected during the discussion in their small group) and by reading appropriate articles in the enrichment magazine.

Then the LifeLight weekly study process will begin all over again!

Recommended Study Resources for John

Concordia Self-Study Bible, New International Version. St. Louis: Concordia Publishing House, 1986. Interpretive notes on each page form a running commentary on the text. The book includes cross-references, a 35,000-word concordance, full-color maps, charts, and time lines.

Lenski, R. C. H. *The Interpretation of St. John's Gospel.* Minneapolis: Augsburg Publishing House, 1963. This older volume is a reliable, comprehensive, confessionally sound commentary by a Lutheran theologian.

Luther, Martin. Sermons on the Gospel of St. John. *Luther's Works.* Edited by Jaroslav Pelikan. Vols. 22–24. St. Louis: Concordia Publishing House, 1957, 1959, 1961.

Morris, Leon. *The Gospel According to John,* NICNT. Grand Rapids, MI: Wm. B. Eerdmans Publishing Co., 1971. Rated by Dr. Erich Kiehl as perhaps the best commentary on John: "demonstrates a wide and careful knowledge of the total content. Written in a simple style with many valuable excursuses."

Roehrs, Walter R., and Martin H. Franzmann. *Concordia Self-Study Commentary.* St. Louis: Concordia Publishing House, 1979. This one-volume commentary on the Bible contains 950 pages and is tailored for lay use.

Westcott, B. F. *The Gospel according to St. John,* Grand Rapids, MI: Wm. B. Eerdmans Publishing Co., 1950 reprint. An old standard; a helpful resource.

Every Voice a Song Pipe Organ Accompaniment for 180 Hymns and Liturgy. St. Louis: Concordia Publishing House (order no. 99-1565). Use this music CD for worship hymn accompaniment.

Using Overhead Transparencies

Some lecture leaders like to use the overhead projector. Others find it to be more a hindrance than a help. We recommend that you use an overhead or a chalkboard to show at least the outline of each lecture.

For those who would like to experiment with further use of an overhead projector, use the blacklines in the Appendix of this guide to make overhead transparencies for the lecture in session 1. To make transparencies for use on your overhead projector, simply place the blackline masters on a copy machine and hand-feed plastic transparency sheets, one for each blackline master. (Note that there is one transparency for each one or two sections of the lecture.) The overheads can help the lecture leader stay on track, enhance interest, and still allow for flexibility in the oral presentation.

As your time and interest in this approach permit, follow the same pattern for the lectures in sessions 2 through 9.

The Messenger Is the Message

John 1:1–18

Preparing for the Session

Central Focus

God became a human being in order to make Himself known to us and to establish a personal relationship with us.

Objectives

That participants, by the power of the Holy Spirit working through the Word,

1. become increasingly aware that the Jesus whom they will meet in the Gospel is God in person, communicating His love to them;

2. receive Him in joyful and grateful faith as they experience Him in Word and deed;

3. grow in their personal relationship with Him as they participate in His life and ministry.

Note for small-group leaders: Lesson notes and other materials you will need begin on page 61.

For the Lecture Leader

You get to put the frosting on the cake. After that you get to put candles on it, light them, and lead the celebration. The high point of that celebration is when you serve a big slice of that delicious cake to all participants.

In a sense, they make the cake. By their individual study and small-group discussions of God's Word, they gather the ingredients, mix them, and bake the cake. Your delightful privilege is to help them all to enjoy it. You review the content of the portion of John's Gospel they have studied. You beautify and enrich it with additional information and interpretation. Then you invite and encourage them all to feast on it, to taste its goodness and sweetness, to take it with them into their daily lives.

That can be a very rewarding and exciting experience, if done well. And you can do it well. Those who plan and prepare this LifeLight Bible study material and the participants who use it are supporting you with prayer. You will want to approach your lecture each week fortified by your own prayer as well. One way God will answer that prayer is through your careful personal study. Be sure to work through the daily assignments thoughtfully, so that you are dealing with God's Word in the same way that individual participants are.

Once you have done that, you are ready to prepare your lecture presentation. Your goal as you go about this is to make the material your very own by whatever method works best for you. The following procedure should be helpful.

1. *Reread the section of John* on which your presentation is based, asking the Holy Spirit to open your mind and heart so that you discover in these verses everything He wants you and the others to have.

2. *Read through the entire lecture presentation* in this leaders guide in a single sitting, without stopping to underline or make notes. This will give you a sense of the whole discussion.

3. *Reread the lecture,* this time very slowly, underlining a few of the most important points in each section and making brief notes that summarize the main thoughts.

4. *Restate the lecture in your own words,* if at all possible. Either rewrite the lecture completely or prepare an outline from which you can give your own version.

5. *Prepare for delivery* by saying your lecture aloud, going over each section several times, and referring to your notes as little as possible. Then, after reviewing your notes or manuscript, practice saying the whole thing several times. As much as possible, say it from memory and from your heart in your own words and way, with as much eye contact as possible. Be enthusiastic, personal, and concerned about your hearers, rather than about yourself and how well or how poorly you might be doing.

6. *If you choose to read the printed lecture,* practice reading

it aloud until you can do it comfortably and naturally, making whatever word changes are necessary. For ideas on how to emphasize and express things in the printed lecture, listen to the cassette tape for this course available from CPH. If some small groups meet at other times during the week, provide them with an audio recording of your presentation or the cassette mentioned above.

7. *Get feedback* from a few participants whose judgment you value. Ask them for suggestions that will enable you to do an even better job.

8. *Use an overhead projector.* This is a wonderful teaching aid. It helps you to get your message across, reinforces it visually, and maintains the interest of your hearers. If you are not accustomed to using an overhead, consult with a pastor or a teacher for hints on making the best use of it.

Session Plan

Worship

Begin the session with the hymn and prayer printed in the study leaflet. Accompaniments are available in denominational hymnals, such as *Lutheran Worship* (refer to hymnal index). Note: Concordia Publishing House has available *Every Voice a Song*, a 9-CD set of organ accompaniments for 180 hymns and liturgy. All the initial worship hymns in the LifeLight courses are included in this resource. It's especially helpful for mission congregations and small parishes. See the list of study resources on page 7.

Lecture Presentation

1 The Prologue Is the Key That Unlocks the Gospel of John

The Gospel of John is a marvelous part of Scripture—beautiful, rich, moving—if you open it up with the key provided by the author in the opening verses. Verses 1–18 of chapter 1 are that key, usually called the prologue. In these verses the author offers us some vital information about the person whose story he is about to tell—who this person is, why He came, and how we should react to Him.

2 The Author Is Jesus' Best Friend

Before we consider this important introductory material, it will help us to know who the author of this Gospel is. Of course, in the highest sense of the term, the author is God. Through the power of the Holy Spirit, God gave John the thoughts and words as well as the desire to write. However, when the Spirit caused the biblical authors to write, He worked through their personalities, experiences, and interests. So, it is important for us to know something about the human author as well.

How interesting and even exciting to know that the John who wrote this Gospel was Jesus' best friend! There are five references in this book to "the disciple whom Jesus loved" (13:23; 19:26; 20:2; 21:7, 20). Important Christian leaders writing soon after the New Testament age identified him as the one who wrote this Gospel. He is the brother of James and the son of Zebedee. James and John, along with Peter, were the inner circle of the Twelve. Peter, James, and John were often the only disciples with Jesus on special occasions—the raising of Jairus's daughter, the transfiguration, and the Maundy Thursday night of prayer in the Garden of Gethsemane. Of these three, John was the one to whom Jesus felt drawn most strongly in personal friendship.

Many details in the Gospel indicate that its author was someone very close to Jesus and was personally involved in the events he describes. That person was almost certainly John. John and his brother James were fishermen from the vicinity of Capernaum on the north shore of the Sea of Galilee. **If available, indicate these places on a map.** They were partners in this business with Simon Peter and Andrew.

Not long after his first meeting with Jesus, John returned to his home and to his job, fishing in Galilee. There he and Jesus met again. This time Jesus called John, James, Peter, and Andrew to be His disciples. They left their boats and nets and families, and for the next three years they were His inseparable companions.

Why did Jesus and John become best friends? The Bible doesn't answer that question. There is no reason to believe that John was any better than the other disciples. Like the rest of the disciples, John was usually slow to understand the meaning of what Jesus said and did.

And yet, there was something about him that Jesus appreciated and enjoyed. Jesus was a real human being—like you and me. It's not always easy to understand and explain why people become good friends. In some cases, it is because they are much alike. In other cases, it is because they are so different. Opposites can attract, and that may be the case with Jesus and John. When John refers to himself as "the disciple whom Jesus loved," this does not mean that Jesus loved him *more* than the other disciples, but rather that He loved him *differently*—as a friend.

The result is that we have an opportunity to get better acquainted with Jesus with the help of His best friend. John wrote many years after Jesus' ascension into heaven. Since his readers already had the Gospels of Matthew, Mark, and Luke, John emphasized teachings and activities of Jesus *not* covered in these earlier writings. We can imagine Christian people 50 or 60 years after Jesus' time saying, "John, you knew Him better than anyone else. You were His best friend. Tell us what He said and did as *you* remember it and as *you* experienced it." Moved by the Holy Spirit, John wrote this amazing account of the life and work of his best friend.

3 John Uses Simple Terms with Deep Meaning

John, in his writing style, uses simple picture language to convey deep meaning. We run across many of these little words that express big ideas already in the first verses of the prologue. John is telling us about a person, isn't he? Verse 2—"He was with God"; verse 3—"Through Him all things were made." Then look down to verse 10—"He was in the world." And in verse 17 John gives us His name: Jesus Christ.

Notice the terms John uses to describe Jesus. Jesus is called (v. 1) "the Word" and (v. 9) "the true light." In verse 4 John declares, "In Him was life." These are common, simple terms, but exactly what are they telling us about Jesus? Verses 1–2—Let's start with the first descriptive term. Jesus is the Word, the Word who was with God in the beginning, the Word who *was* God. And then in verse 14 we are told that this Word became flesh and made His dwelling among us.

4 The Messenger Is the Message and the Sender!

What is a word, any word? In a way, a word that you speak or write is something of *you* sent to someone else. Jesus is the Word of God, John explains. God wants to say something important to us human beings, and He is saying it through Jesus. However, Jesus is more than the messenger. He is also the *message.* Not only what Jesus said, but everything that He did and experienced tells us about God. However, the full truth is even more remarkable than this. Verse 2—Jesus is not only God's messenger and God's message, He is also God Himself—the *sender* of the messenger and the message: "The Word was God."

In what sense is Jesus God? In verse 34 John the Baptist identifies Him as the Son of God. In 3:16 Jesus refers to Himself as "God's one and only Son," (3:13) who was sent from heaven (3:17) to save the world. Although all believers are God's children, Jesus is God's Son in a unique way. Verse 2—He has been God's Son from all eternity, "was with God in the beginning." A human son comes from his parents and comes after them. God's Son always was. When the term *Son* is applied to Him, it describes a relationship rather than His origin, for God's Son had no beginning. As a human being He had a beginning when He was conceived and born, but as God's Son He always existed.

A child is a completely separate being from his or her parent. God's Son and the heavenly Father are one being (10:30): "I and the Father are one." And yet, there is a difference, a distinction between them. The Son and the Father talk to each other (12:27; 17:1–26). The Father loves the Son (Mark 1:11; Luke 3:22) and the Son obeys the Father (John 15:10). So, although they are one being, they are two persons who relate to each other and communicate with each other. This is one of the ways in which God is much more complex than we human beings are. Each of us is just one person. God is three persons—Father, Son, and (to make it even more interesting and challenging!) Holy Spirit as well. One God in three persons—that's what we mean when we describe God as the Holy Trinity.

Something important to keep in mind is that in each person we meet the whole Godhead (14:9): "Anyone who has seen Me has seen the Father," Jesus explains.

And He adds (16:12–15) that the Spirit will share the blessings of both Son and Father with those to whom He speaks.

All this is rather difficult to understand and explain, but it is also important. Unless we recognize both plurality (three-ness) in God as well as unity (one-ness), much of what we are told in this Gospel will be very confusing.

5 God Communicates by Becoming One of Us

Just think about this for a moment. The almighty God, the mind and power behind the entire universe, wants to communicate with us human beings. He wants us to get to know Him. He wants to share His feelings and hopes and dreams for us. He has some important things to tell us—important to Him as well as to us. Because they are important, He came in person to speak to us and He came as one of us. The man Jesus is God communicating with us in person as a human being like ourselves. If you want to know about God, if you want to know God personally, John is telling us, look at the man Jesus. Listen to Him. He is the living Word of God. Verse 14—"The Word became flesh and made His dwelling among us." Without in any way giving up His deity, His divine nature, and without becoming sinful, God became a real human being—as human as you and I.

6 Jesus' Communication Reveals and Conceals

While in the world in human flesh and form, Jesus lived life on the same terms that we do, without any special privileges or protection. Most of the time He did not use His divine powers. When He did use them to perform miracles, it was never for His own convenience or advantage. Rather, His actions were done to help people and make them aware of God's great love for them.

Verse 14—"We have seen His glory, the glory of the One and Only, who came from the Father." Verse 18—"No one has ever seen God, but God the One and Only, who is at the Father's side, has made Him known." When Jesus spoke and performed miracles, especially when He died and rose again, people recognized the power and love of God in Him. That is what the term *glory* means. It is the presence and compassion of God in a tangible and visible form.

God revealed Himself clearly and beautifully in the man Jesus. But strangely enough, in a certain sense He also concealed Himself—because He came as a true human being. Our sinful pride asks, "How can we accept this helpless baby of Bethlehem—this carpenter's son who grew up among us—as God Himself, come to save us?" Also today: "How can it be that through the simple water of Baptism and the bread and the wine of the Lord's Supper we receive His forgiveness?" During Jesus' earthly life and ministry, as well as today, people can and do reject Him and refuse to see God in Him.

Jesus is the light of God shining in the darkness of this world. He can drive away the darkness of our ignorance. He can overcome the blindness of our unbelief. However, we are free to turn toward the darkness, close our eyes to the light, and choose not to recognize Him. For us to recognize God in Jesus and to trust Him requires a miracle of revelation and conversion. But we can—and by nature do—always refuse Him by ourselves. Thank God, then, for the miracle of conversion, by which God's own Spirit turned our hearts from unbelief to faith and led us to "receive" Him and thereby become children of God. 1 Corinthians 12:3: For "no one can say, 'Jesus is Lord,' except by the Holy Spirit."

7 The Heart of the Message: God Loves Us

What is it that God is saying to us through Jesus? The answer is encouraging. The heart of the message is that God loves us more than we ever imagined, even though we don't deserve His love. All that Jesus said, did, and endured conveys this good news. Verse 17—"Grace and truth came through Jesus Christ."

Grace is love that helps those who are unlovable. Grace is patience and care for those who are disobedient and disappointing. Grace is generously forgiving and doing good to those who actually ought to be punished.

In the Ten Commandments, which God gave through Moses, God tells His redeemed people how they are to live. Because of our sin, we do not live up to God's standard. Through Moses and other Old Testament writers He also promised to rescue us from the consequences of our sin. God kept those promises when Jesus came. That's what the term *truth* means in John's Gospel— God's faithfulness to His promises. This helps us to understand verse 17: "For the law was given through

Moses; grace and truth came through Jesus Christ." In other words, God loves us even though our sins offend Him. He loves us and deals with our sinfulness through Jesus, just as He promised He would.

8 The Purpose of God's Communication Is a Close Personal Relationship

As we get to know God better through Jesus, we will appreciate Him more, respect Him more, and trust Him more. Through Jesus, God shows Himself to be like an incredibly kind man or woman of great resources who approaches a group of corrupted and degraded street youth. They have no future, no hope. But this person in love approaches them and says, "I care about you and want to help you. I can take you out of all this. If you will let me, I will adopt you as my children with all the advantages and privileges that this involves." Jesus establishes and sustains a close personal relationship with God, a beautiful parent-child relationship.

Then in verse 4 John says, "In Him was life and that life was the light of men." *Life,* as used by John, refers to the condition of a human being in a personal, saving relationship with God. In Jesus, God creates and nourishes this life.

As we walk with Jesus, listen to Him, and talk with Him in this study of John's Gospel, expect it to happen. Look forward to it eagerly. Enjoy the prospect and the experience of a closer, more meaningful faith relationship with God through this remarkable person whom John presents to us.

Concluding Activities

Offer a prayer asking God to bless the study of all those who are participating in this LifeLight course. Pray that God would guide and bless the efforts of all those who are serving as leaders.

Make any necessary announcements. Distribute the enrichment magazine and encourage participants to read it as part of their weekly study. Then distribute study leaflet 2.

Notes

Notes

Introducing the Messenger

John 1:19–2:25

Preparing for the Session

Central Focus

At first Jesus is introduced by others, and then He introduces Himself.

Objectives

That participants, by the power of the Holy Spirit working through the Word,

1. realize that then and now Jesus chooses to be introduced by others;

2. accept the high privilege of directing others to Him;

3. are attentive and responsive when others direct them to Jesus;

4. eagerly anticipate personal encounters with God as they study and share Jesus through the Gospel of John;

5. because of their faith relationship with Jesus, recognize God's love at work in His creation in both ordinary and miraculous ways;

6. respond with humility and contrition when the loving God expresses judgment on them for their sins.

Note for small-group leaders: Lesson notes and other materials you will need begin on page 65.

For the Lecture Leader

How did your first presentation go? Probably you experienced some anxiety and disappointment. You may also have experienced the excitement of having God's Word come alive for you and for your hearers.

In order to keep improving, it is important to evaluate each presentation. Review in your own mind what went well and try to figure out why. Analyze the attention patterns of your hearers. During what parts of your presentation did they seem most interested? How did they react to your use of the overhead projector? How smoothly and comfortably did you use this teaching aid? Were you able to maintain good eye contact? Did you express things in your own words?

Obviously, questions like these will also help you discover and understand what did not go well. As you identify things that need to be fixed, don't be too hard on yourself. It was your first presentation in this series. Even very experienced, professional presenters keep noticing things that they could do better. Be confident that God's Spirit accomplishes great things through even our imperfect efforts.

Discuss the presentation with your feedback person or group. Start with the positives. Ask for comments about things that were most effective and why they seemed to be effective. Also ask for suggestions for improvement. Try not to be hurt or defensive about these suggestions. You asked for them, and they are being offered in order to help you.

Then, as you prepare your next lesson, try to do even better the things that went well last time. In other words, keep building on your strengths. Of course, you will also want to address weaknesses.

Pick out one or two of these that seem most important and most easily corrected, and do your best to improve there. Don't try to fix everything at once.

Above all, approach your study of this new portion of John's Gospel with eager anticipation. Follow the preparation steps recommended last week. Remember that your high privilege is to introduce Jesus to your hearers. They already know Him, but you can help them to meet Him again, to gain fresh, new insights into who He is, what He has done, and what He means to them. As you study and teach about Him, you will meet Jesus in person yourself. Your faith in Him and your love for Him will grow. He will mean more to you than ever before.

For the Director

Here's a checklist for you:

- Make sure study leaflets for the next session (session 3) are handed out at the end of this session.
- Attendance taking, a procedure for collecting funds to pay for study materials, and training and feedback sessions for other LifeLight leaders should also be in place by this time.
- Make sure that small-group leaders of the home groups are using good quality tape players for the taped lectures.
- Listen for any problems the other leaders may be encountering so they can be remedied quickly.
- Remember to pray for LifeLight leaders each day.

Session Plan

Worship

Begin the session with the hymn and prayer printed in the study leaflet. Accompaniments are available in denominational hymnals, such as *Lutheran Worship* (refer to hymnal index), or on the *Every Voice a Song* CD set.

Lecture Presentation

1 Introduction: God's Son, His Living Word, Needed to Be Introduced

When God's Son became a human being, He lived in this world for 30 years, and only a few people (His parents; shepherds at His birth; Wise men; Simeon and Anna) realized who He was! When it was time for Him to begin His public ministry, He had to be introduced. No doubt because of His sinlessness and devotion to the Father and His love for people, others realized that He was quite special, but they didn't realize how special.

You see, up to this point (age 30) Jesus had never used His divine powers. He performed no miracles, did no preaching or teaching. Jesus' deity was hidden by His humanity. Friends and acquaintances, even close relatives, did not know that He was the eternal Son of God in human flesh.

Even during His public ministry, when He spoke and acted with the power of God, Jesus did so with restraint. People could choose not to recognize God in Him. That is also true today. By now it is far more evident than it was then that He is the God and Savior of all people. He has made this known through His death for our sins, His victorious resurrection, the sending of His Spirit, and the remarkable spread of His church. However, clear and convincing as all this is, people can still ignore Him or reject Him.

That is why at the beginning of His ministry, and even today, God's messenger, Jesus, needs to be introduced. He relies on those who have recognized Him and believed in Him to direct others to Him.

2 John the Baptist Introduces Jesus (1:19–36)

The first one to introduce Jesus publicly as the promised Savior was a very remarkable person himself. He was a cousin of Jesus, born miraculously to his parents in their old age. From the day of his birth, he had been designated as the one who would prepare the way for the Christ. Most of his life had been spent in the desert, where God strengthened and shaped him specifically for his vital role.

John the Baptist had a striking appearance and powerful message. With long, shaggy hair and beard and rough camel's hair clothing, he wandered around the area near the Dead Sea preaching to whoever would listen: "Get ready, the Christ is near, confess your sins and accept the cleansing of baptism. Anyone who is not ready when He comes will receive terrible judgment." Although he preached in the desert, his fame spread. So impressive was he that many began to think that John himself was the promised one. Verse 19—When representatives of the Jewish leaders approached John, they wanted to know whether he was the Christ. Immediately and emphatically John denied being either the Christ or any of the Old Testament prophets who were expected to appear prior to His coming. "You don't know Him," John informed them, "but He is already here. He is the great one. I am only His lowly servant."

How do you suppose John felt about answering that way? He had been the center of attention and was a celebrity to whom people were drawn magnetically. He could have become the head of a powerful movement.

However, instead of accepting that kind of attention and expectations for himself, John discouraged them and directed their hopes to another.

Later, perhaps that same day, Jesus came to John to be baptized. John was confused by this. Although he did not know for sure, he apparently suspected that his cousin Jesus was the promised Savior. But, if He were that, why would He need to be baptized? Baptism was for sinners. The Christ could not be a sinner. Jesus insisted that John baptize Him, and it was then that it happened. God had given John a sign by which he would be able to identify the Christ with certainty. The sign was that the Spirit would come down on Him in the form of a dove.

While Jesus was being baptized John saw this happen. Then, as if that were not enough, he also heard the Father's voice from heaven say (Matthew 3:17), "This is My Son, whom I love; with Him I am well pleased."

Then, the very next day while they were talking, John saw Jesus walking toward them. "This is the one I was telling you about," he exclaimed. "Since we talked yesterday, God showed me that He is the one whom we are waiting for. Look, the Lamb of God, who takes away the sin of the world."

This way of referring to the Christ must have surprised these Jews. They thought of the promised Savior as a conquering king, not as a sacrificial lamb. They expected Him to save them, the Jews, not the whole world. But John had it right. His introduction of Jesus was absolutely on target. God's Son came to save everyone, and He would do it by giving Himself into a sacrificial death on the cross. Apparently, those to whom John first introduced Jesus reacted negatively. For they soon became enemies, determined to kill Jesus.

One day later John the Baptist introduced two of his own disciples to Jesus—Andrew and another. Andrew is specifically mentioned in verse 40. Since John (the author) was a close associate of Andrew and gives such a full description of what happened, we assume that he was the unnamed disciple mentioned in verses 35–37. Even though it meant that they would leave him to be with Jesus, John the Baptist pointed his two disciples to Jesus, and they now left John and attached themselves to Jesus.

John the Baptist is a beautiful example of how all of us can and should introduce others to Jesus. By what we say and do, we want to call the attention of others to this great messenger of God. We want them to realize who He is and what He has done, and then accept Him by faith. The faithful witness will say as John did, "I'm not the one you need. Jesus is. Follow Him."

3 A Chain Reaction: New Followers Introduce Others to Jesus (1:37–51)

These new followers, in turn, introduced others to Jesus. In time, they introduced others, and then still others, and so on and on down through the ages until we were also brought to Jesus. When we were baptized or brought to faith by the witness of a Christian friend, we were introduced to Jesus. Now it is our high privilege and responsibility to keep that chain reaction going, to keep introducing new people to Jesus. Then those people will introduce others and so on and on until Christ returns.

Andrew's experience with Jesus is fascinating. When John the Baptist pointed to Jesus and said to Andrew and the other disciple (probably John), "Look, the Lamb of God," they fell in step right behind Him and spent the rest of the day with Him. As they became acquainted with Him and listened to Him, Andrew realized that this new friend whom John called "the Lamb of God" was the Messiah (that is, the Christ, the promised Savior). Andrew was overwhelmed. For many hundreds of years, in fact since Adam and Eve fell into sin, God's people had been waiting for this person, this Messiah, to come. And now He was here. His name was Jesus. Andrew knew Him personally.

He could not wait to share this wonderful news, and he started with his own brother and business partner, Simon. Verses 41–42: "The first thing Andrew did was to find his brother Simon and tell him, 'We have found the Messiah' (that is, the Christ). And he brought him to Jesus." That is the place for all of us to start, with those nearest and dearest to us. First we should approach those among our families, friends, acquaintances, business associates, or others who do not know Jesus and introduce them to Him. The good news of Christ flows most effectively through our close personal relationships.

Introducing his brother Simon to Jesus may be the most important service Andrew ever rendered. He seems to have been a very ordinary person of modest abilities. And yet, the brother whom he introduced to Jesus became an outstanding Christian leader of great boldness and lasting influence, someone who brought thousands to Jesus. You and I can find a great deal of encouragement in this. We, like Andrew, may be quite ordinary. However, God may use us to bring to Jesus others who will be extraordinary in their service to Him.

The chain reaction continues. Soon after His contact with Andrew, Jesus met a friend of Andrew named Philip. Probably Andrew had also said something to Philip about Jesus and had told Jesus about Philip. For when Jesus was about to leave Judea and return to His home in Galilee, he looked up Philip and invited him to come along.

Philip accepted the invitation without hesitation. Before beginning that journey to Galilee, which was also Philip's home, Philip visited with Jesus and discovered for himself who He was.

Full of excitement over his discovery, Philip eagerly looked up his friend Nathanael and told him the good news. Verse 45: "We have found the one Moses wrote about in the Law, and about whom the prophets also wrote Jesus of Nazareth, the son of Joseph." Friend introducing friend—that's the way saving faith is spread most naturally.

Nathanael was skeptical. He couldn't imagine anyone so important coming out of insignificant Nazareth. But Philip insisted that Nathanael come and meet Jesus in person before deciding against Him. When they met, Nathanael was overwhelmed. Jesus greeted him as though He already knew him. He referred to Nathanael's skeptical response in a friendly, almost amused way. In effect, Jesus said, "You say what you think, don't you, Nathanael? And apparently you are not impressed by what you hear about Me."

Nathanael couldn't understand how Jesus knew what he said or how he felt before they ever met. Jesus added to his astonishment when He explained that He saw him sitting in the shade of a fig tree before Philip found him. This was apparently quite a distance away and would have required the use of divine power.

That did it! Verse 49—Nathanael's skepticism collapsed, and he made a marvelous confession of faith: "Rabbi, You are the Son of God; You are the King of Israel." Jesus

accepted his statement of faith, but in a loving and amused way chided him for his initial skepticism. "You haven't seen anything yet, Nathanael. Wait till you see heaven open and angels coming back and forth on Me."

We may find skepticism, too, in those whom we want to introduce to Jesus. But a first negative reaction doesn't mean someone will always feel that way. Philip's way of handling skepticism and resistance was effective. He didn't argue with Nathanael. He simply repeated his invitation. "Don't take my word for it. Meet Him yourself and then decide."

4 Jesus Introduces Himself as Lord of Creation (2:1–11)

Up to this point Jesus relied on others to make Him known. Now the time had come for Jesus to make Himself known, and He chose to do this with actions. So that people could realize that He was God's Son and the promised Savior, Jesus began to do things that only God could do.

Soon after, Jesus and His new friends returned to Galilee. **If available and convenient, refer to a map.** There they were invited to a big wedding party, where a serious problem arose. The wine ran out. The celebration had hardly begun when the servants ran out of the only beverage they had to serve. The bride and groom and their families could have been thoroughly humiliated.

For some reason, when the servants realized what had happened, they shared this information with Jesus' mother, Mary. Or, maybe she overheard the servants as they were discussing it. Verse 3—In any case, Mary told Jesus, "They have no more wine." Better than anyone else, she knew who Jesus was. But He had never performed a miracle before. Did she expect Him to do one now? Verse 4—Jesus' response is rather puzzling. "Dear woman, why do you involve Me? . . . My time has not yet come." In other words, "What am I supposed to do about this? Do you really think that this is My big chance to show who I am?" His comment to His mother sounds almost disrespectful, like a put-down. But Mary didn't take it that way. She turned to the servants and said, "I don't know what He may ask you to do, but whatever it is, do it!"

Jesus did ask them to do something. Pointing to six

huge stone jars, each holding 20 or 30 gallons, He said, "Fill those jars with water and then take some of it to the man in charge of the banquet." When the master of the banquet tasted it he was astonished and a bit angry. He called the bridegroom over and said: "What is this? Where have you been hiding this good stuff? We should have served this first and saved the cheaper wine until now when the guests have already had some and are no longer so particular."

God's Son performed His first miracle. He did something that only God could do—He turned water into wine! He had shared in the work of creation (1:3) at the beginning of time when the world was made. Now He takes control of a small part of that creation (180 gallons of water) and, without touching it or even saying a word, quietly changes it into delicious wine. In this way He introduced Himself as God's Son and the Lord of creation.

However, only a few of the many people present even knew that it had happened! The servants, Mary, and the disciples knew of the miracle. It was an important experience for the disciples. As a result, they put their faith in Him. The faith begun when they first met Him down in Judea was greatly strengthened by this display of His divine glory.

From time to time Jesus also reveals Himself to us as the Lord of creation. Do we notice this when it happens? Has your food or money ever stretched farther than you expected it to? Have you or has anyone close to you ever recovered from sickness or injury in a surprising way? Have you ever been headed for a disastrous automobile accident and then at the last second missed it by inches?

When things like this happen to us, we often just breathe a sigh of relief and go on. But these experiences are too important for that. If we bother to notice, we will recognize our Lord's divine glory in them. He shows that He is the Lord of glory in our lives too.

5 Jesus Introduces Himself as the Lord of the Temple (2:12–22)

In the next scene we see Jesus in quite a different setting. With His disciples He makes the journey south again. **If available, indicate on map.** They go to Jerusalem to celebrate the feast of the Passover. All Jewish men were required to be at the temple in Jerusalem for this occasion.

When Jesus came into the temple with His disciples, He acted as though He owned the place. Merchants and money changers had filled the temple court to sell to the worshipers—at sky-high prices—animals and birds for sacrifices. The place was noisy and smelly. How could people worship God properly in the midst of all these distractions? Jesus became angry and decided to do something about it. He made a whip out of ropes and drove them out with all their livestock.

He upset their tables and scattered their coins. And He did all this with such confidence and authority that no one tried to resist Him. Verse 16—"Get these out of here!" He said. "How dare you turn My Father's house into a market!"

By this startling public protest Jesus indicates that He is the Lord of the temple, because He is the Son of the God whose temple it is. Although they did not resist His bold action, some disputed the bold claim. They demanded a miraculous sign to prove that He had the authority to say and do these things. Verse 19—Jesus said, "Destroy this temple, and I will raise it again in three days." They couldn't believe their ears. It had taken 46 years to build the temple, and He said He would rebuild it in three days? Nonsense! But He was talking about the temple of His body.

In just a few years He was going to offer His body as the sacrifice for the sins of all people. All the animal sacrifices performed in the temple day after day and year after year were a shadow and a promise of the great, final, completely effective sacrifice that Jesus would become on the cross. Remember (1:29), John the Baptist introduced Him as the "Lamb of God, who takes away the sin of the world." Here Jesus suggests that as the Lord of the temple, He Himself will finally take the place of that temple as the focus of the worship of God's people. He will die as the Sacrifice to end all sacrifices—and then rise again to prove that He is all that He claimed to be.

In our worship today as we study His Word and receive His Supper, we meet this same Jesus. He visits our "temples" too. Often He is disturbed by what He finds. Much goes on to distract from our communication with Him and strains our relationship with Him. He comes with judgment for all of this. But, above all, He comes with mercy. He says, "I have paid for your sins with the sacrifice of Myself. I will not hold them against you. I want to be closer to you. I want our friendship to grow. I want to be the most important person and the most important influence in your life." It is an offer too good to refuse.

Concluding Activities

Ask participants to take a moment to think of one person to whom they might introduce their Savior. Then ask each person to pray silently, asking the Holy Spirit to help them introduce Jesus to that person.

Make any necessary announcements, briefly mention again the resources in the enrichment magazine, and distribute study leaflet 3.

Notes

One-on-One

John 3:1–4:42

Preparing for the Session

Central Focus

Jesus communicates powerfully with two very different individuals, inviting and drawing them into a personal and saving relationship with God.

Objectives

That participants, by the power of the Holy Spirit working through the Word,

1. recognize that the God of the universe communicates and relates intimately with them as individuals;

2. are prepared to receive from Him even more than they expect;

3. make the focus of their faith Jesus, as He in love gives Himself for the life of the world;

4. reach out to others and invite them into a one-on-one relationship with Him.

Note for small-group leaders: Lesson notes and other materials you will need begin on page 69.

For the Lecture Leader

One of the most important factors in making your presentation effective is your personal enthusiasm. If you have discovered something important for yourself and for your life in chapters 3 and 4, and if you are excited about this, your hearers will notice and their interest will rise. Enthusiasm is contagious. Even tired and distracted listeners "come alive" when the presenter is genuinely enthusiastic about what he or she has to share.

Enthusiasm can be indicated in various ways. Sparkling eyes and animated speech, choice of words and tone of voice, gestures and rate of speech—all can signal enthusiasm.

This does not mean that to be effective every presenter must be a bubbling, emotional personality. A more reserved and quiet person may express enthusiasm more subtly, but it will show, and it will make a big difference to the hearers.

Where do you get this enthusiasm? Enthusiasm for God's Word comes from God's Word. As you study the conversations between Jesus and these two very different people, enter into these conversations yourself. Let Jesus speak to you personally about your need for Him and the miracle of His saving love for you. Discover in His approach to Nicodemus and the Samaritan woman how you might reach out to those who are still apart from Him. Think deeply about the high privilege you enjoy of being in a personal relationship with God through Him. Enter into all of this with fresh interest, as though you had never heard any of this before.

And be enthusiastic about the opportunity to share this with your hearers. Concentrate on them and on this exciting message from God's Word. Set aside concern about yourself.

Enthusiasm cannot be faked, but it can and will be cultivated as you personally become involved in the message.

Session Plan

Worship

Begin the session with the hymn and prayer printed in the study leaflet. Accompaniments are available in denominational hymnals, such as *Lutheran Worship* (refer to hymnal index), or on the *Every Voice a Song* CD set.

Lecture Presentation

1 Introduction: God's Son Deals with Us as Individuals

The God of all the universe and of all people deals with us as individuals. Jesus makes that very clear in the experiences recorded in chapters 3 and 4. Jesus is the eternal Son of God through whom all things were made. He has ruling authority over everything and everyone.

And yet, He loves us individually. Individuals who come in contact with Jesus receive more from Him than they expect. Nicodemus was looking for information. The Samaritan woman was looking for an inexhaustible water supply. Instead, Jesus offered them both something infinitely more valuable. He offered them Himself and eternal life, which only He can provide. The same is true today. People look to Jesus for all kinds of things—health, happiness, wealth, success. And, Jesus often gives them what they seek. But above all, Jesus wants to give people Himself and eternal life, which only He can provide.

2 Jesus Accepted Nicodemus as He Was

Nicodemus sensed something special in Jesus. Only the great prophets of the Old Testament, such as Moses and Elijah, performed miracles. Perhaps Jesus was as great as they. Nicodemus felt it was worth exploring further. On the other hand, being seen with Jesus did not seem advisable. After all, many of the other Jewish leaders became hostile to Jesus when He drove the merchants and moneychangers from the temple and claimed that He could rebuild that temple in three days (chapter 2). These enemies of Jesus were friends of Nicodemus. There was no need to offend them. So, Nicodemus arranged to visit Jesus at night.

Jesus knew what Nicodemus was thinking and how he felt (2:25) "for He knew what was in a man." So, Jesus knew that Nicodemus was reluctant, perhaps even ashamed, to be publicly identified with Him. But He accepted Nicodemus as he was.

Jesus always accepts people as they are when they become interested in Him. This is the case even when their interest is mixed with embarrassment or when their expectations are low. Although He is the almighty eternal Son of God, Jesus is not too proud to reach out to such people. He will not turn away from anyone who is at all open to Him.

Sometimes we underestimate how interested in Jesus and open to Him people like Nicodemus are. Because

they are important, educated, or successful, we assume they would not care to know more about Jesus. But, given the right opportunity and invitation, they may respond with surprising eagerness.

3 Jesus Offered Nicodemus More Than He Expected (3:1–21)

In his opening remarks to Jesus, Nicodemus expressed a high opinion of Jesus. He regarded Jesus as way above himself, as someone whom God had sent in an unusual way. Nicodemus undoubtedly also knew John the Baptist, but realized that Jesus was even greater than John. John himself had made that very clear.

Jesus' reply, however, startled Nicodemus. Nicodemus came looking for information and, instead, Jesus offered him the kingdom of God and new life. Nicodemus came looking for a teacher sent from God. Jesus identified Himself as the Son of God who is also the Son of Man, the Messiah spoken of in Daniel and in the other prophets. Nicodemus was looking for someone who could enlighten him. Jesus explained that He would die for him and for the whole world. Nicodemus wanted new knowledge from God. Jesus offered a relationship with God that would make him a new person. Nicodemus was expecting a great deal from his contact with Jesus, but what he found far exceeded his expectations.

Jesus explained that the kingdom of God is something that happens inside a person. It happens when the Holy Spirit rules and directs people from within. Not outward political or military power, but inner influence in individuals is what the kingdom of God is all about. Through the water of Baptism as well as through God's Word, the Holy Spirit reaches people and establishes His rule within them. He does this not by force, but by persuasion. He gives them new attitudes—faith in God, love for God, desire to please and honor God. The Spirit energizes them to serve and obey God. In short, He makes them new persons. They are born again—born from above as loving, obedient children of God, as loyal citizens of God's kingdom.

Obviously, Nicodemus was puzzled. He thought Jesus was speaking of physical birth, but Jesus pointed out that He was referring to something else. Verse 6—"Flesh gives birth to flesh." Birth from our human parents does not bring us into the kingdom of God. It only brings us into the sinful, condemned, dying human race. Only a second birth from the Spirit can bring us into the kingdom of God. The Holy Spirit does this invisibly but powerfully—like the wind. You can't see Him as He works in hearts and minds bringing forth new children of God. But He is there, and it happens. The child of God is born again of water and Spirit through Holy Baptism. God uses the earthly element of water, the physical agent of cleansing, joined with the Word, which brings the presence and power of the Holy Spirit. The Spirit gives us faith, which receives God's cleansing forgiveness. There is one Baptism, the washing of water with the Gospel Word.

Jesus was increasingly emphatic as He responded. In effect, Jesus said, "Nicodemus, you ought to be able to grasp this. A lot of what you have learned in Scripture points to this. I am telling it to you straight. I am not making this up. I bring it to you from heaven, from God Himself. Believe Me, this is the way it really is!"

From those important and jolting introductory statements Jesus moved boldly into the very heart of the matter. Jesus is the Son of Man and the Son of God, who was sent from heaven. In order to rescue people from their sinful, dying condition, He would be hung on a cross to die. He is the ultimate expression of God's love. He is God's love in action. God cared enough for this world full of sinners to send His very best. He sent His one and only Son. Through what He did and endured, those who were orphans and outcasts from God become His children. They can be born again into a relationship with Him that will never end. Yet many continue obstinately to refuse Him and turn away. And, sadly, they shall throughout eternity suffer the consequence of their unbelief—eternal separation from God.

4 John the Baptist Became Less So That Jesus Could Become Greater (3:22–36)

The ministry of John the Baptist continued even after he publicly identified Jesus as the Christ (1:29–35). He continued to preach and to baptize. However, John and what he was doing became less and less important as Jesus' ministry grew. John expected this and accepted it.

Verse 31—"I, on the other hand," John explained, "am just a human being—'from the earth.'" "I am here to testify to Him and direct others to Him. I am not disappointed that others are going to Him instead of coming

to me. He is God's great attraction, not I."

In the faithful, unselfish witness of John the Baptist, we have a marvelous example for ourselves. The focus of the faith we have and are to share is Jesus Christ. Faith is recognizing and receiving Him as God's forgiving love in human flesh and form. It is counting on Him and Him alone as the one who can bring us into a close and everlasting relationship with God.

5 Jesus Unexpectedly Reached Out to a Samaritan Woman (4:1–38)

Not long after His one-on-one conversation with Nicodemus in Jerusalem, Jesus and His disciples headed for home in Galilee. His unusual success in attracting followers had stirred up unfriendly concern among the Pharisees. At this point Jesus did not want a confrontation with them. So He left for a time. Then came the first surprise. Instead of going around Samaria on the way back to Galilee, Jesus led His disciples through Samaria. Most Jews would not do this. They despised Samaritans. Although Samaritans had some Jewish blood and parts of Jewish religion, they were a mixed ethnic group. Jews regarded them as mongrels and were strongly prejudiced against them.

Jesus, however, did not feel that way toward Samaritans. He accepted and respected them. One of His most moving parables featured someone whom we now call the *Good* Samaritan (Luke 10:30–37).

It was about noon when they arrived at a resting place by Jacob's well. Jesus remained there while His disciples went into the nearby village of Sychar to get some food. It was then that another surprise happened. A Samaritan woman came to draw water, and Jesus spoke to her. Jews didn't like to talk to Samaritans. Jewish religious teachers did not ordinarily talk to women in public, even Jewish women. But the real surprise was that Jesus asked her for a drink of water from her container. Jews regarded Samaritans as unclean. This meant that by drinking from her container, Jesus would temporarily be considered unfit to participate in Jewish acts of worship.

The woman was well aware of all this and was shocked by His request. Why did Jesus do this? What kind of statement was He making to her? He was saying: "I don't look down on you Samaritans the way other Jews do. I'm not afraid that you will contaminate Me. I am interested in you. I want to associate with you and talk with you. I want to be your friend. And I would like to have you do Me a favor."

Jesus knew very well that one of the best ways to get better acquainted and even make a friend is to ask a stranger for a favor. It was an astonishing message for a Samaritan woman to receive from a Jewish teacher. She was hardly ready for that and did not handle it very graciously.

But Jesus was not put off by her defensive reply. Perhaps with a smile on His face and a twinkle in His eye Jesus said that He could do her a great favor in return. In other words, "If you give me some of your well water, I will give you living water." The more Jesus said the more bewildered this woman became. Perhaps her thoughts went something like this: Does He mean that He will draw from the deepest part of the well where it is fed by an underground spring? She blurted out her objections.

Jesus replied with a still more puzzling comment. He made it clear that the water He referred to had nothing to do with this well or any other well. The water He had to offer satisfied a much deeper and more urgent thirst. It satisfied the need for God and for eternal life. Furthermore, once you drank this water, He said, it would stay inside you and become a spring that produced an inexhaustible supply. You would never be thirsty again. Verse 15—Still thinking that He was talking about physical water, the woman said, "Sir, give me this water so that I won't get thirsty and have to keep coming here to draw water."

If Jesus wasn't referring to physical water, to what was He referring? Sometime later, in another connection, Jesus explained. Whether she realized it or not, this woman was thirstier than Jesus was. She was dying of thirst for God. Jesus was offering to meet that need, as only He could. Although the Samaritan didn't understand everything this strange Jewish teacher was saying, something very important was happening between them. They were communicating. Jesus was communicating acceptance, interest, respect. Although surprised and confused, she was responding with interest.

Jesus decided it was time to go deeper. He let her know that He was fully aware of her sordid past. In a straightforward but loving way He called attention to her sins—

her five broken marriages and present immoral relationship. She sensed from this that He must be a prophet. Doesn't this remind you of Nathanael's reaction (1:48–49) when Jesus revealed information about him? To have a prophet of God discussing her sins was not a comfortable position for her. So, she did what most people do in such circumstances she changed the subject—to questions about worship.

In reply, Jesus in effect said, "Oh, yes, worship! That's the heart of the matter, all right! What is most important about worship is not so much where you do it, but how you do it. God wants us to communicate with Him openly and honestly."

Verse 17—"I have no husband." Perhaps thinking about her earlier unsuccessful attempt to conceal her sinful relationship from this prophet of God, the woman once again became uncomfortable. She changed the subject again. She seems to have been saying, "Oh, well, I guess we can leave all these hard questions for the Messiah to answer when He comes." Verse 26—But Jesus persisted. He used her statement to make a very explicit and powerful claim. "I who speak to you am He [the Messiah]."

Jesus' approach to this woman is a model of witnessing. He affirmed her value by starting a conversation and asking a favor. He stimulated her interest, dealt with her need for God, and offered to meet that need. He listened to her and related His remarks to what she had said. Everything in His manner and words was designed to make her glad that she had met Him.

6 She Brought Many from Her Village to Jesus (4:39–42)

Her response to Jesus was quick and dramatic. She believed His claim and ran back to the town to tell others about Him. Imagine the surprise of the townspeople! This sinful woman, probably a social outcast, breathlessly announced to them whom she had met and what had happened. Rather than telling them outright that He was the Christ, she invited them to come and meet Him. Verse 29—She raised a thought-provoking question: "Could this be the Christ?" They couldn't resist. Often it is better to stir up someone's curiosity about Jesus and extend an invitation than to give a long speech. The people of the town took her seriously and began to make their way to the well.

Meanwhile, the disciples had returned with some food. They were surprised to see Him talking with a woman but did not discuss it with Him. They found Him in a state of excitement. He was not interested in the food they brought Him. But He was thrilled at the response of this woman, at her faith and eagerness to share it. He sensed that there would be a great harvest from the Gospel seed He had sown in her heart, which she was now scattering in the town. He challenged His disciples to prepare for that harvest.

Harvest time came quickly. When the townspeople found Jesus, they persuaded Him to stay with them and teach them more. A great many believed. Having heard it from Jesus Himself was even more convincing than hearing it from the woman. Perhaps the disciples helped Jesus teach these people. Or, perhaps they only observed. In any case, the disciples experienced the great joy of the harvest. The time would come when they would become active and effective in gathering people to God. We, too, can experience the joy of the harvest.

Concluding Activities

Ask participants to think of someone they know who does not yet believe in Jesus. Then ask them to imagine themselves somehow sharing their faith in Jesus with that person. Finally, ask them to pray silently that God would enable them to do what they had imagined themselves doing.

Make any necessary announcements. Remind participants to check the enrichment magazine for materials that will, indeed, enrich their daily study. Then distribute study leaflet 4.

Notes

Notes

Communication through Healing

John 4:43–5:47

Preparing for the Session

Central Focus

Jesus communicates divine love by compassionately responding to the need for healing.

Objectives

That participants, by the power of the Holy Spirit working through the Word,

1. discover in Jesus' healing activity (both miraculous and natural) that the God of the universe cares about their suffering and losses and is willing to do something about them;

2. confidently ask for help when they face such needs;

3. notice and gratefully celebrate His answers to prayer for such help;

4. trust that if God does not give them what they ask for, He will give them something even better;

5. acknowledge penitently their negligence in asking for His help and/or in giving thanks for His marvelous response to their needs;

6. interpret every act of His physical care as an expression of His saving love.

Note for small-group leaders: Lesson notes and other materials you will need begin on page 73.

For the Lecture Leader

To what extent are you making the lecture material in this guide your own? The leader's guide is designed to help you prepare your presentation. It suggests an outline, interpretation, and illustrations. And it can be very useful to follow the lecture in the manual rather closely. However, this will be most effective if you first make it your own.

This involves reading it carefully and thinking about it deeply so that you clearly understand the material. Do this early in the week so you can consult your pastor or some other knowledgeable person if you have questions.

After you understand the printed lecture, rework the language wherever necessary. Use your own expressions where those of the author don't sound natural when coming from you. Put things in your own words as much as possible.

Perhaps the most important way to make it your own is to include your own experiences in the presentation. You may have a wonderful experience of healing to share whether through a miracle or through the marvels of modern medicine. God may have helped you at a time of trouble, even before you asked Him to. Or, you may have neglected to praise and thank Him for His help. This can add greatly to the interest of your presentation. It will also identify what you say as your presentation.

A word of caution. From the example of John the Baptist (chapters 1 and 2), we learned that the goal of the witness is to direct attention to Jesus, not to self. Even when we include our own experiences, we want to do this in such a way as to glorify Him and not to call attention to us.

By including yourself in the presentation, you are making some important statements: I need Him too. I believe Him and take Him at His word. This applies to my life and can apply to yours as well.

The more you make the presentation your own, the more it becomes your witness rather than just a lecture. Your conviction and sincerity do not have the power to make people believe and obey—only the Holy Spirit can do that! However, they can stimulate the interest and attention of your hearers. When that happens, your hearers may be more open to God's Word, the Holy Spirit's instrument as He works in minds and hearts.

Not only your hearers, but you yourself will enjoy the presentation more if you make it your own.

Session Plan

Worship

Begin the session with the hymn and prayer printed in the study leaflet. Accompaniments are available in denominational hymnals, such as *Lutheran Worship* (refer to hymnal index), or on the *Every Voice a Song* CD set.

Lecture Presentation

1 Introduction: Every Experience of Healing Is an Experience of God's Loving Care

Have you or has anyone close to you ever experienced a miracle of healing? If you get into a discussion of remarkable cures in even a small group of Christians, someone is likely to have one to report. "The doctor said she had cancer and only six months to live. Six years later she was alive and well, and the doctor was dead."

What has happened in cases like that? We Christians believe that God has gotten involved in the lives and bodies of such people. We believe that the God who creates all things can and does heal the damage that sin brings upon His creatures. Most often He does this through the natural healing processes of the body or through medical treatment. However, He is not limited to these means. He is able and willing to act directly and powerfully through miracles.

He does not always do this, even when people beg Him desperately to do so. For good reasons God may withhold healing—both natural and miraculous. Paul was a staunch believer and a great missionary. God used him to perform miracles for others. But when Paul sought healing for his own illness, God answered that He would give him something even better than healing. He would give him grace—a marvelous experience of God's loving support. That would enable him to bear his suffering and even to benefit from it. It would also prepare him to help others in their suffering (2 Corinthians 12:7–10; Romans 5:1–5).

The point is that every time you experience healing, you experience God's presence, power, and love. It may be recovery from some minor complaint, such as a cut finger or a head cold. Or it may be from something major and life-threatening, such as a heart attack or cancer. It may take place through treatment or through a miracle. However and whenever you experience healing, either in yourself or in someone you love, you are experiencing an act of God.

2 Someone Comes to Jesus for a Miracle (4:43–47)

After His brief missionary visit among the Samaritans, Jesus returned to his home region of Galilee. The people were excited about His return, because (2:23) some of them had seen the miracles He had performed at the Passover Feast in Jerusalem. Here we see how God's purposes in miracles of healing can be frustrated. People tend to become more interested in the miracles than in the loving God who performs them.

Ordinarily God gives miraculous help to those who already recognize Him and believe in Him. By an unusual experience of His love and power He wants to strengthen their faith relationship with Him. He does not want to dazzle or entertain people with magic. He wants to be their Savior and friend. When miracles accomplish that, He is happy. When they get in the way of that or become a substitute for that, He is disappointed.

Verse 46—While in Galilee Jesus visited Cana again. One person in particular was thrilled to learn that Jesus was there. He was an officer in the king's service whose son was dying.

Imagine how he felt. There was no other hope for his son, whom he loved deeply. Probably he had accepted the fact of his death and with a heavy heart was just waiting for it to happen. Then the word reached him: Jesus, the man who had turned water into wine, was in the area! Suddenly there was hope after all. Although he lived some distance from Cana, he hurried to Jesus and begged Him to come and heal his son.

Exactly what he said to Jesus is not recorded. But from Jesus' answer it seems to have been something like this: "Sir, I know You can do amazing things. I have a son whom I love, and he is going to die. Please come and heal him."

3 Jesus Creates Faith with No Strings Attached (4:48–54)

Verse 48—Jesus' reply reveals His frustration and disappointment with the general attitude and mind-set of the Galileans. He says, in effect: "If I do this miracle, you will believe? Are you offering your faith only in response to a miracle of healing?" Jesus was not trying to give this desperate man a hard time. Rather, He was trying to help him believe in the right way. Jesus may encourage faith with miracles. He may reward faith with miracles. But He refuses to buy faith with miracles.

We may sometimes find ourselves trying to bargain with the Lord. "If only You will get me out of this trouble or miraculously solve this problem, I will believe and obey You more than ever before."

Verse 49—The official apparently accepted Jesus' words, meant to kindle his faith, and was not discouraged. "Sir, come down before my child dies." This was not yet the faith Jesus wants to see in us. But, at least, a serious obstacle to faith had been removed. Jesus was more than willing to grant the request. Verse 50—To the officer He said, "You may go. Your son will live." Then, the miracle of a genuine faith (the greatest miracle of all) began to happen. Verse 51—The man took Jesus at His word. He expected the healing to occur. And, before he reached home, someone met him with the good news. His son had recovered! The fever had left him quite suddenly the previous day early in the afternoon. That was the exact time that Jesus promised it would happen.

Now the miracle of healing had its intended effect. The man responded with genuine faith. He realized that Jesus was more than a wonder-worker. He recognized Him as His loving, caring, powerful God. And, as he shared all this with the other people in his home, they too believed.

The application to us is clear and encouraging. Jesus welcomes our request for help, even for miraculous help. But He doesn't want us to bargain with Him. He can and does grant our requests, as He sees fit, with the hope that we will recognize God's loving care in this help and that our faith will grow as a result.

4 Jesus Does an Unexpected, Unrequested Miracle of Healing (5:1–8)

In chapter 5 the scene changes abruptly from Cana in the north to Jerusalem in the south. **If available, indicate on a map.** Jesus returned to that holy city for one of the major religious feasts. We are not told which one. While in Jerusalem He came to the pool of Bethesda. We cannot know for certain whether the remarkable healings attributed to this pool actually happened or whether people only believed they did. This point hinges on whether verse 4 was part of John's inspired text or was inserted later. The verse is not in the earliest and most reliable manuscripts of John's Gospel. According to this verse, from time to time the water in that pool was stirred by an angel. The first sick or disabled person who could get into that pool after the water was stirred would be cured.

Many people in need of healing waited at the pool for their opportunity. Jesus began a conversation with one who had been an invalid for 38 years. For much of that time he had been waiting at the pool for his chance. But since he could not move quickly without help, he never could get to the water in time. He had great confidence in that water, great hopes that if only he could get into it at the right time, his troubles would be over. He was encouraged by the interest of this friendly stranger. Perhaps He would agree to wait around and help him into the water when it was stirring.

What happened next to this invalid was an incredible and unexpected surprise. Verse 8—Jesus said, "Get up! Pick up your mat and walk." Immediately strength and health surged into his weak and withered body. He was cured instantly and completely. Before he could even say thanks, Jesus slipped away. Overwhelmed with astonishment and joy, the man began to stroll through the streets of Jerusalem, carrying the mat on which he had lain as an invalid for so many years.

Not everyone was ready to celebrate this great blessing. Some were upset and critical. According to their traditional interpretation of God's law, the man should not have been carrying his mat on the Sabbath. Furthermore, whoever did it should not have performed an act of healing on the Sabbath. On other occasions, too, Jesus had provoked hostile reactions from Jewish leaders by healing on the Sabbath (Luke 6:6–11; 13:10–16) and answered His critics very effectively. On this occasion they did not realize at first that Jesus was the healer, because the man who had been healed had no idea who his benefactor was.

Sometime later Jesus located the man in the temple. He may have gone there to thank God for the healing. When they met, Jesus issued a serious warning: Verse 14—"See, you are well again. Stop sinning or something worse may happen to you." Jesus here points the man to a need greater than physical healing—the need for forgiveness of sin and spiritual life. He seeks to lead the man to faith in Him as the Savior.

It's possible, too, that Jesus had some particular form of sin in mind, perhaps a sin that had brought on the man's ill health. That is sometimes, but not always, the case. In John 9:1–3 Jesus makes that clear. For example, the person who sins sexually or abuses drugs may contract AIDS. This terrible disease may be a consequence, even a divine punishment, for specific sin. In another case, someone may innocently contract the same disease through a blood transfusion.

To the unbeliever, every sickness, accident, or tragedy is an expression of God's anger for sin—whether recognized as such or not. To the person with saving faith in Jesus, all sins are forgiven. That means that sicknesses, accidents, and tragedies even if they are consequences of specific sins—are not punishments from God. Since Jesus was already punished for our sins, God will not punish us for them a second time. To the believer, such afflictions are a loving correction from God and an invitation to accept the wonderful support of His grace. He promises to turn such troubles into a blessing (Romans 8:28; 2 Corinthians 1:3–7).

Pondering what he had been told, the man who had been healed went back to those who had criticized him for carrying his mat on the Sabbath. He told them that Jesus was the One who had healed him. As we will see, this turned them violently against Jesus.

5 Jesus Claims Divine Sonship and Authority (5:16–18)

When they met Him face-to-face, His opponents accused Jesus of breaking the Sabbath. Verse 17—His reply was startling, "My Father is always at His work to this very day, and I, too, am working." In other words: "It's all right for God to work on the Sabbath. It's people who are supposed to rest on this holy day. And, since I am His Son, I can work on this day too." In chapter 2 we noted that Jesus revealed Himself as Lord of creation and as Lord of the temple. Now He insists that He is also Lord of the Sabbath.

His enemies understood the full meaning of His claim and they were infuriated. In claiming to be God's Son, Jesus was claiming to be God's equal. This was the beginning of a conflict and a conspiracy that eventually led to Jesus' arrest, torture, and death.

6 Jesus Supports His Claim with Powerful Testimonies (5:19–47)

Again and again in the speech He made to His critics, Jesus insists that He is God's Son and that He has all the authority that goes with this. Verses 19–20—He sees all that the Father does and participates in it. Verses 21–23—He will raise the dead at the end of time and be the judge of all. Verse 23—He deserves the same honor that the Father receives. Verse 24—He provides eternal life to all who believe in Him. These are astonishing, staggering claims. The anger and resistance of His enemies mounted as Jesus said these things.

But Jesus did not back down. Neither did He walk away from them. He loved these people, too, and was going to die for them. Verse 18—He realized that before too long they would succeed in their efforts to kill Him. Amazingly, the death He would die at their hands was to pay for their sins and the sins of us all. As He continued His conversation with them, Jesus tried to persuade them that what He said was true. Verse 34—He hoped that at least some would believe and be saved.

To those who were offended and angered by His claims, Jesus said, in effect, "Before you make your rejection final, consider the evidence. Notice the impressive testimonies that support My claim."

Jesus continues (vv. 33–45), "John the Baptist bore witness to Me. Although I don't rely on mere human witnesses, what John said about Me was true. You had a lot of respect for him. Why not take him at his word in what he said about Me? God the Father is My main witness. He is the One who sent Me into the world on this great mission. In the Scriptures, the writings of Moses and the prophets, He promises My coming and indicates what I will be like. You think a lot of these Scriptures and study them constantly, but you miss their main point, their main message. It is a message that testifies to Me."

But even as He is talking with them, Jesus senses that

their hostility and unbelief are unshakable. Regretfully He informs them that in rejecting Him, the Son whom God sent, they are also rejecting God. Verses 41–44— There can be no love for God in the hearts of those who refuse to accept His Son. Jesus is hurt and offended by their rejection. And yet, He explains that He is not going to accuse them before the Father. That will not be necessary. It is Moses who will accuse and condemn them. For in his writings, Moses had prepared them to recognize and believe in Jesus. But they ignored this part of Moses' message.

What a tragedy! They did not recognize God's presence, love, and power in Jesus' miracle of healing. Instead they found reasons to criticize and hate and reject Him. It is another example of something we have noted in several previous lessons. Jesus does not force Himself on anyone. Instead, He invites us to believe. With words and mighty works He encourages and enables us to believe. Thank God that, by His grace, we do believe and that we, too, know the healing power of Jesus!

Concluding Activities

Ask participants to think for a moment about how God has cared for them. Perhaps the Lord has cared for some of them by healing or preserving them in a remarkable way. After a moment of silent reflection, have everyone join in singing the Common Doxology ("Praise God, from Whom All Blessings Flow"). Since not all participants may be familiar with this hymn, you may want to write the words on a transparency, chalkboard, or newsprint sheet or distribute copies to all.

Make any necessary announcements and distribute study leaflet 5.

Notes

Notes

Life-Giving Communication

John 6:1–71

Preparing for the Session

Central Focus

After miraculously providing food for five thousand, Jesus offers Himself as a life-giving feast.

Objectives

That participants, by the power of the Holy Spirit working through the Word,

1. count on Jesus to multiply their resources and deal with the crises in their lives;

2. cherish Him, above all, for His life-giving sacrifice;

3. stand by Him faithfully even when others desert Him;

4. seek and accept His pardon for their mistrust, unbelief, and faithlessness.

Note for small-group leaders: Lesson notes and other materials you will need begin on page 76.

For the Lecture Leader

Something remarkable happens when you make your presentations, telling the people about Jesus—who He is, what He did and said, what He's like. As you talk about these things, Jesus Himself joins the group; through His Word Jesus is present. Through His Word Jesus Himself speaks to the hearts of your hearers.

Isn't that exciting? Your high privilege is not only to make people aware of Jesus, but actually to put them in personal contact with Him. This doesn't happen when you're talking about anyone else. For example, if you were talking about Martin Luther, your words would not bring Luther to the scene. If you spoke very well, he might seem to be present. You might describe him

vividly and make him seem real. But, in fact, Luther would not be present.

However, when you speak about Jesus, in your presentations or anywhere else, He is right there in person—with all of His love and power. Through the Holy Spirit He gets through to people and helps them in the ways that they need most. He forgives them and changes them. They are built up in their faith. They are given the desire and ability to become more Christlike. They are sustained in their hold on eternal life.

I am sure that your class would be impressed if Jesus appeared in visible form while you were talking. Although He does not appear visibly, He is present for and through every presentation. He speaks and acts through you, through His Word that you share. You can be confident about your presentations, knowing that He is there.

Session Plan

Worship

Begin the session with the hymn and prayer printed in the study leaflet. Accompaniments are available in denominational hymnals, such as *Lutheran Worship* (refer to hymnal index), or on the *Every Voice a Song* CD set.

Lecture Presentation

1 Introduction: Jesus Traveled from North to South to Minister to All of God's People

If available, use a map for the following introduction and at appropriate places in the lecture.

Have you noticed that John's account of Jesus' ministry moves back and forth between south and north? Chapter 1 describes events in the south—Judea. Chapter 2 begins in the north—Cana of Galilee and then shifts abruptly to Jerusalem in the south, where He cleansed the temple, and, in chapter 3, conversed with Nicodemus. Chapter 4 takes place in Samaria, midway between Judea and Galilee, and concludes with Jesus back in Cana of Galilee. Jerusalem is the setting for chapter 5. Our lesson for this session is based on chapter 6, which once again occurs in Galilee.

From this we may draw several significant conclusions. One is that Jesus traveled a lot. He had important work to do, important messages to bring to all of God's people. He needed to communicate with people in the very center of Jewish life and religion—Jerusalem. But He also needed to communicate with people at the outer edges of the Jewish nation—Galilee.

Another conclusion we may draw is that John is not attempting to tell everything Jesus said and did. He tended to concentrate on things not covered so completely by Matthew, Mark, and Luke. For example, of the eight miracles reported in John's Gospel, only the two described in this chapter are also recorded by the other evangelists.

Jesus' miracle of feeding the five thousand is the only miracle reported in all four Gospels. However, here John includes some details and a great deal of discussion the others do not.

2 Jesus Provides Food for Five Thousand (6:1–15)

The magnetic attraction of Jesus' miracles of healing was growing ever stronger. Mark 6:30–35 tells us He and His disciples looked for peace and quiet away from the crowds. However, the curious and excited crowds found them. It was late in the day. People were hungry. Jesus was concerned for the hungry people and challenged the disciples to address the problem. Verse 5—"Where shall we buy bread for these people to eat?" He did not ask, "Shall we try to feed them?" Instead He asked, "How are we going to do this?"

The problem was a big one: no place to buy food, not enough money. Andrew called attention to a young boy whose mother had remembered to pack a lunch. Verse 9—Andrew was almost embarrassed to mention the lunch, but he did, adding, "but how far will they go among so many?"

With that tiny lunch Jesus fed that enormous crowd. Verse 10—The number five thousand refers only to the men. Counting women and children, there were proba-

bly more than ten thousand appetites to satisfy. And satisfy them Jesus did. By His divine power Jesus miraculously multiplied those meager resources so that there was enough for everyone and then some. Verse 13—What was left over was many times more than what they had started with!

Now the people were really excited! Verse 4—It was almost Passover time. They were thinking a lot about how God, through Moses, had delivered their ancestors from slavery in Egypt and how He had fed their ancestors with manna during their 40-year trek through the desert.

What Jesus had just done was a lot like that. He was another prophet-leader like Moses. Just imagine—with Him as king it would no longer be necessary to work to put food on the table! Sensing what was on their minds, Jesus dismissed the crowd and went to a mountainside to pray. He had something more important to offer than free sandwiches, but that was all they could think about.

3 The Miracle Has Meaning for Us (6:1–15)

Through this miracle Jesus has much to say to us. What He wants to communicate is both comforting and challenging. By providing food for so many people, He is telling us that He cares about the physical needs of people. He is saying, "I know what it's like to be hungry or to be hurt. I'm human too." Confronted by our physical needs, or anyone else's, His heart goes out to us. And He is eager to act. He is not satisfied just to feel sorry for us. He wants to help. This is reassuring. We don't have to talk Him into caring and helping. He's aware of our need and ready to respond even before we ask.

There is also an exciting challenge in this miracle. When He was ready to help these hungry people, Jesus involved His followers. He got His disciples to struggle with the problem. He took the lunch of that little boy and used it. Do you suppose the boy offered his lunch to Jesus? Or did Jesus request it? In any case, Jesus used His followers and their resources to meet the needs of others. He puts that same challenge before us. There is a whole world full of hungry people, and Jesus says to us as He said to His disciples then (Mark 6:37), "You give them something to eat."

As we face that overwhelming challenge, we are encouraged by this miracle. From it we discover that God can do a lot with very little. All He used to feed that great multitude was the lunch of one child! When we realize all that needs to be done in this world or even in our own communities, we feel terribly inadequate. Our resources seem hopelessly insufficient. But Jesus says, "Give Me what you have, and I will multiply it. I will produce benefits beyond your wildest dreams."

4 Jesus Provides a Rescue at Sea (6:16–21)

After feeding that great crowd, Jesus dismissed them and told His disciples to go ahead of Him by boat back to Capernaum. He needed to be alone with His heavenly Father. It was evening.

When the boat was far from shore, a strong wind came up. The waves grew high, and the disciples were struggling to keep the boat from capsizing. In the midst of all this danger they were terrified to see someone or something walking toward them on the water. They thought it was a ghost. Verse 20—But when the figure came closer, they heard a familiar voice calling out to them over the noise of the wind and the waves, "It is I; don't be afraid." They were relieved and delighted as He joined them in the boat. With Him there the waves and the wind did not seem so threatening. In fact, they died down almost immediately. Before they knew it, they were safely on shore. What a difference it made to have Jesus join them in the middle of this crisis! (See Mark 6:45–51 for additional details of this incident.)

Jesus is also ready and willing to join us in the crises that we face. He is always nearby. He says to us, as He said to them (Mark 6:50), "Take courage! It is I. Don't be afraid." With Him at our side we can face the worst storms and stress that come upon us. And we can be sure that He can control and change anything that threatens us. He is the God of the universe, the Lord and Master of all creation.

5 Jesus Is the Bread of Life (6:22–40)

When daylight came, the crowd whom Jesus had fed realized that He was gone. When a fleet of boats landed on the shore where they were, they got in the boats and headed for Capernaum to search for Jesus.

Verse 25—When they found Him, they asked how He had crossed the sea without a boat. Jesus didn't bother to answer that question. Verse 26—Instead, He expressed His disappointment in their motives. "You went to a lot of trouble to find Me," He said, "just because I fed you with bread and fishes. That food didn't sustain you very long, did it? By now you are hungry again and want some more. I have something better than bread and fish to offer you. I have food that will keep you going forever. That is really worth working for."

"What do we have to do in order to get that food?" they asked.

"Believe in the One God has sent," Jesus replied, referring, of course, to Himself.

Verses 30–31—"You want us to believe in You, trust in You, follow You? Well, then, You'll have to show us that You are the real thing. You fed us once. Moses, whom our forefathers followed, fed them regularly for 40 years. If You do that, we'll be happy to believe in You."

Verse 32—Jesus challenged their statement that Moses had provided bread from heaven. It was God who had provided the manna, not Moses.

At this point Jesus becomes clear and emphatic (6:34–40): "Do you understand? I am the bread of life. If you receive Me by faith, you will have eternal life. You will be in a loving, saving relationship with Me and with My Father. And that relationship will never end. Even death will not end it. For at the Last Day I will raise you up again. My Father wants you to have all this. He sent Me to tell you about this life and to bring it to you. If you accept Me, I will see to it that you never lose this life."

What Jesus said to them, He also says to us. He says that He Himself is God's most important gift to us. Food and other material things, which He provides, are important. But they cannot meet our most urgent need—the need for eternal life. Jesus alone can do that.

6 Jesus Answers His Critics (6:41–59)

Some in the crowd began to grumble at Jesus' high claims. They are referred to as "the Jews." In John's Gospel this expression usually refers to the Jewish religious leaders who were so hostile to Jesus. These people challenged what He had said. Verse 41—"We know where this man came from, and we know His family. How can He say that He is the bread that came down from heaven?"

Jesus would not back down. "Stop grumbling and listen to Me. The Father wants to draw you to Himself through Me. If you listen to Me and accept Me, you will have everlasting life. I am the bread of life, the bread that will enable you to live forever. Take Me by faith. Eat this bread of life, and you will live forever."

Then Jesus added something that really shocked His critics. Verse 51—"This bread is My flesh, which I will give for the life of the world." Jesus was referring to His sacrificial death on the cross.

Verse 52—"How can this man give us His flesh to eat?" His enemies protested angrily.

Jesus replied (vv. 53–58), "Unless you eat My flesh and drink My blood, you do not have life. If you do eat My flesh and drink My blood, you have eternal life. And I will raise you on the Last Day. Manna kept people alive only for a short time. If you feed on Me, you will live forever."

7 Eat His Flesh and Drink His Blood (6:41–59)?

What exactly is Jesus talking about when He says that we must eat His flesh and drink His blood? The first thing that comes to our minds is Holy Communion. In that Sacrament Christ gives us His true body and blood to eat and to drink. Is this what He is referring to here?

No. He spoke these words quite some time before He instituted His supper. To His hearers on this occasion any reference to Holy Communion would have been quite meaningless. In this conversation, eating His flesh and drinking His blood refers to something else. It refers to faith.

He is urging His hearers to accept Him and to value Him above everything else, even above the free food He had provided. He wants them to count on Him and His forthcoming sacrifice for eternal life. To feed on Him is to believe in Him.

But although to His original hearers these words did not point to Holy Communion, to us they may. For we know what they could not know. We know that His life-giving sacrifice, His very body and blood, are given to us

in that sacrament. When, trusting in His promises, we eat the bread and drink the wine of Holy Communion, we eat and drink His body and blood for our pardon and eternal life.

8 Jesus Is Deserted by Many Disciples (6:60–71)

Verse 60—Not only Jesus' enemies, but also many of His disciples choked on these words. "This is a hard teaching. Who can accept it?" they said. Jesus was aware of their discomfort and unbelief, but He didn't back down from them or try to soften His statements. In fact, He gave them something even harder to think about. Verse 62—"So, you think it's preposterous that I am God's Son who came down from heaven to give My flesh for the life of the world. You don't think I can give My flesh to eat and My blood to drink, do you? What if you were to see Me go back into heaven again? Then what would you think?" To those who were astonished by something Jesus said, He often gave them something even more astonishing to think about.

Verse 63—Then Jesus went on to explain what enables a person to believe. It is the Holy Spirit. Through Jesus' words the Spirit touches the heart and creates faith and gives them life. He brings them into a living, saving, personal relationship with God that will never end. People cannot believe on their own. "The flesh counts for nothing." Only by the power of the Holy Spirit can they believe.

However, God does not force anyone to believe. Even those close to Jesus, even those who heard and knew His Word, could reject Him and His Word. Verses 63–64—"The Spirit gives life . . . yet there are some of you who do not believe," Jesus observed. Verse 66—"From this time many of His disciples turned back and no longer followed Him," the evangelist notes.

What could be more tragic than to have the opportunity to believe and to reject it? What is more pathetic than for someone who once believed and followed Jesus to turn away from Him? And yet, it can happen. It could happen to us. Although we may not give in to it completely, we are all guilty of many "little" desertions and betrayals of Jesus.

After many others had left Him, Jesus turned to the Twelve. "How about you? Do you want to leave too?"

He asked them. Verses 68–69—Simon Peter gave a magnificent reply, "Lord, to whom shall we go? You have the words of eternal life. We believe and know that You are the Holy One of God." Although Peter meant to speak for the others as well as for himself, Jesus knew that one of the group, Judas, was not only going to desert Him, but would actually betray Him to His enemies. Faith and unbelief were standing side by side, even among His closest followers.

We need to confront our own weakness, mistrust, and unbelief. We need to approach Jesus with all of this and confess it sorrowfully. Then we can claim His generous promise of forgiveness. He is our sacrifice for sin. That is something we can count on. He is the bread of life from heaven. As we feast on Him by faith, our sins are forgiven, and we will live with Him forever. The pressure to leave Him is very strong. Things in and around us make us want to turn away in unbelief. But, forgiven and strengthened by His grace, we can stand by Him faithfully, no matter who else may desert Him.

Concluding Activities

Express a brief prayer thanking God for the faith in Jesus that the Holy Spirit has given to us. Ask God to strengthen that faith through this LifeLight Bible study of John's Gospel.

Then make any necessary announcements and distribute study leaflet 6.

Notes

Notes

Communication Breakdown

John 7:1–8:30

Preparing for the Session

Central Focus

Despite Jesus' very explicit testimony supported by mighty deeds, those in the best position to accept Him refused Him—a tragic breakdown in communication.

Objectives

That participants, by the power of the Holy Spirit working through the Word,

1. realize that they can and at times do spoil communication from the Lord and His attempts to relate to them;

2. reach out patiently and lovingly to others who are not responding to the Lord's communication with them;

3. point out the forgiveness He offers to those who tune Him out;

4. joyously take advantage of the communication opportunities Jesus provides.

Note for small-group leaders: Lesson notes and other materials you will need begin on page 79.

For the Lecture Leader

As a teacher of God's Word you have a limited but very important role. Essentially, your task is to get and keep people's attention.

You don't have to think up any new information. It's all there for you in the Bible. The presentations in this manual help you to lift that information from the Bible, explain it, and apply it to your hearers. That can be quite a challenge, of course. But think how much more difficult it would be if you had to invent new ideas and truths and stories every week. As it is, you need simply to discover these things in the Bible and figure out a good way to share them.

You don't have to make people believe God's Word or obey God's will. The Holy Spirit does that. All you have to do is present God's Word and will in such a way that people will take it seriously.

Or, to put it another way, your purpose in teaching is to make people aware of a very special person, Jesus Christ. This is what the Bible is all about. The ideas, truths, and stories are there to point to Him. As you teach about Him, you bring Him into the minds and hearts of your hearers. You help them to see how He is the answer to their deepest needs. The highest compliment anyone could pay you is to say, "Today in your teaching I saw Jesus."

For this to happen, you need to get their attention and keep their attention. That's all and that's plenty. They will not meet Jesus, they will not grow in faith and obedience, unless they listen. The question you have to keep asking as you prepare and present is "How can I persuade them to listen carefully and thoughtfully? How can I present this material in a way that is fresh and personally meaningful to them?"

Spiritual growth happens when the Holy Spirit gets through the eyes and ears and into the minds of people. Once there He performs miracles of conversion and spiritual development. Getting Him into the learner's mind is the job of the teacher. That doesn't require a miracle. All it requires is effective ways of getting and keeping attention.

Session Plan

Worship

Begin the session with the hymn and prayer printed in the study leaflet. Accompaniments are available in denominational hymnals, such as *Lutheran Worship* (refer to hymnal index), or on the *Every Voice a Song* CD set.

Lecture Presentation

Introduction

In these chapters we see communication breaking down between Jesus and several groups of people. They were people who were in a good position to understand and accept Him. And yet, instead, they misunderstood and rejected Him. Jesus was not the cause of the breakdown. His messages came through loudly and clearly. The cause of the breakdown can be found in the hearers. They misinterpreted His messages and His motives. Out of ignorance or out of envy they refused to take Him at His word.

1 His Own Brothers Did Not Believe (7:1–9)

Between chapters 6 and 7 we have an interval of six months. Chapter 6 took place near the feast of the Passover (v. 4), in the spring. Verse 2—Events in chapter 7 occur in the fall, at the Feast of Tabernacles, a harvest festival. Jesus had been away from Jerusalem for quite some time, perhaps a year or even longer. When He healed the man at the pool of Bethesda, the Jewish leaders were furious. He had done this on the Sabbath. When they challenged Jesus, He claimed to have divine authority to do this. As a result, more than ever before they were determined to kill Him. Jesus realized this and avoided the confrontation. He was not afraid to die. This was His purpose for coming into the world. But it had to be at the right time.

His brothers urged Him to go to Jerusalem and do more miracles there. They thought He was trying to become a celebrity. Jerusalem at festival time would be a great opportunity to get a lot of attention. He ought to take advantage of it.

Perhaps they meant well and thought they were giving Him good advice. However, what they said made it clear that they didn't understand Him at all and that they didn't even believe in Him. Like so many others, they apparently thought that the Messiah was to be a revolutionary hero. If He was the Messiah as He claimed, He ought to be building up the ranks of His followers, they reasoned. This reveals a twisted perception on their part. To regard Jesus as a revolutionary hero is not faith. Faith is trusting Jesus as the Savior from sin and the source of

everlasting life. His brothers were still far from that conviction.

Jesus makes it clear that communication had broken down. Whether they realized it or not, by their unbelief they had put themselves on the side of "the world," that is, on the side of His enemies. They were in no position to give Him advice. They didn't know the right time for Him to make His move.

Can you imagine that? His own brothers seriously misunderstood Him. They had been with Him most of His lifetime. They had marvelous opportunities to listen to Him and to ask Him questions. But their own preconceived ideas of what the Messiah would be like scrambled His message so that they could not receive it.

We, too, can be misled about Jesus by our own preconceived ideas. For example, we might think that, if He loved us, He would always make us comfortable and happy. Or, we might think that there is no way He would ever let anyone be condemned forever. In other words, we try to change Him to meet our expectations, and this, too, is the very opposite of faith.

2 Jerusalem Crowds Misunderstood Him (7:10–13)

When the time was right, Jesus did go to Jerusalem. His enemies, the unbelieving Jewish leaders ("the Jews"), were watching for Him, and people on the streets were talking about Him. Two different views: both of them wrong—were widely held among the common people of Jerusalem.

Verse 12—One was that He was "a good man." This, of course, was correct as far as it went, but still far short of the truth. He was also God's Son sent from heaven to bring life to the world through His sacrificial death. For them to acknowledge Him merely as "a good man" was to bend His message out of shape.

Verse 12—Others took a negative view—"He deceives the people." They heard what He said and, perhaps, even saw what He had done. And yet, they dismissed Him as a fraud.

These comments were not made openly. The Jewish leaders were so violently opposed to Jesus that it wasn't safe to talk about Him publicly, even if one's comments were negative.

3 Jewish Leaders Were Impressed by His Learning but Questioned His Motives (7:14–19)

When the feast was at the halfway point, Jesus appeared in the temple and began to teach. His enemies were impressed by His learning. For someone who had never studied formally under a rabbi, He was certainly well informed. But, from Jesus' comments to them, it is clear that they did not believe in Him. He may know a lot, but His message is not from God. He says what He says in order to promote Himself, to make Himself someone special. By this hostile interpretation of Jesus' words, by questioning His motives, they disrupted all meaningful communication with Him.

But Jesus did not give up easily. He did everything possible to convince them. Even though they were His enemies and were out to get Him, He wanted to help them. "There is a way to find out whether or not I speak for God," Jesus said. "If you do God's will you will find out very quickly."

What does it mean "to do God's will"? In John 6:40 Jesus said, "For My Father's will is that everyone who looks to the Son and believes in Him shall have eternal life." The Father's will is that people believe in His Son. So, Jesus is saying to His enemies, "If you will only try Me, trust Me, believe in Me, you will discover that there is nothing false about Me. You will discover that your suspicions about Me are unfounded. You put a lot of stock in Moses, and he says, 'Thou shall not kill.' Yet, even without giving Me a fair chance, you have decided that you ought to kill Me. Is that the right thing to do?"

In this way our Lord reached out patiently and lovingly to those who rejected Him. This is how we, too, should respond to such people. Our purpose is not to win an argument, but to try to win hearts. We will not always succeed. Even Jesus sometimes failed, as He did in this case. However, we can always try our best, as He did, to restore meaningful communication with those who have turned Jesus off.

4 Pilgrim Crowds Jumped to Conclusions (7:20–24)

Although Jesus' previous remarks were to the Jewish leaders, people from another group may have replied. If so, they jumped to false conclusions about Him. Per-haps these people were pilgrims who had come to the feast from outside Jerusalem. They apparently knew something of what was going on. But they did not know everything. They apparently knew that Jesus had stirred up ill will by healing a man on the Sabbath. But they had heard nothing about a plot to kill Jesus. So, when He referred to that, they concluded He was deluded by an evil spirit. They couldn't take Jesus seriously, because they had jumped to false conclusions about Him.

To them, too, Jesus reached out with gentle persuasion. He didn't bother to reply to their statement about demon possession. Rather He addressed the issue of healing on the Sabbath. "Moses said that a child should be circumcised on the eighth day. And wasn't this done even if the eighth day was the Sabbath? If it is all right to circumcise on the Sabbath, why isn't it all right to heal on the Sabbath? Don't decide about Me on the basis of superficial observation. Don't jump to false conclusions about Me or about what is going on here."

Still today many people jump to false conclusions about Jesus. They make up their minds about Him on the basis of inadequate or inaccurate information. As a result, they end up rejecting a caricature of Jesus and never meet the real person. Communication does not get very far with people who jump to conclusions. Our approach to such people should be one of gentle persuasion, like that of Jesus Himself.

5 Can This Be the Christ (7:25–44)?

What Jesus was saying and doing on this occasion raised questions in many minds.

The common people of Jerusalem were puzzled. "If this is the man the authorities are out to get, why do they let Him speak publicly? Had they decided that He is the Christ, after all? No, that couldn't be. We know where this man came from, and no one will know where the Christ comes from." They were reflecting a wrong opinion, held by some, that Christ's birthplace would be a mystery.

Jesus apparently overheard some of these comments. In effect, He replies, "You may think that you know where I came from, because I now live in Galilee. But before that I came from God in heaven. You don't know Him, but I do, and I came to make Him known to you."

Some in the crowd were outraged by what He said. They wanted to grab Him, and, perhaps, to kill Him. But they could not. God's time for this to happen had not yet come. Others in the crowd reacted differently. They put their faith in Him. Verse 31—They said, "When the Christ comes, will He do more miraculous signs than this man?" Two groups of people heard and saw the same things. Yet saving communication took place with only one group. The other blocked the message. They ended up hostile toward Jesus instead of having saving faith.

By this time the Jewish leaders had had enough. They would stand for this no longer. They sent temple guards to arrest Jesus. Jesus puzzled them with His remarks. Referring to His death, He said that in a short time He would return to the One who sent Him. Then they would not be able to find Him any more. They thought He might be planning to escape Palestine and flee to a Greek-speaking Jewish community elsewhere in the Roman Empire. The guards took no action. They just stood there and listened to Him.

It was the final day of the feast. In the midst of the closing ceremonies Jesus stood up and spoke with a loud voice. He had something important to say to everyone, and He wanted them to hear Him. "If you are thirsty for God, come to Me. I will give you living water, the Holy Spirit. He will not only flow into you, but will flow out from you like a spring-fed stream, to quench the thirst of others." Jesus was thinking about what would happen beginning with Pentecost. Then He would give the Holy Spirit to enable believers to proclaim the Gospel powerfully and convincingly. As a result, through them the Holy Spirit would enable many others to believe also.

Reaction to Him was mixed. Some were well pleased with Him. They thought He must be the Prophet, who was to come in the spirit and power of Elijah to prepare the way for the Messiah. They did not realize that this Prophet had already come in John the Baptist. Others went much further. They realized that He was the Christ. Still others thought they knew better. Unlike the group mentioned earlier, they knew that the Christ was to come from Bethlehem. But they thought that Jesus had been born where He now lived in Galilee. He couldn't be the Christ, they reasoned, because He wasn't born in Bethlehem. How wrong they were! But, convinced that

they were right, they wanted to seize Him and silence Him. To their surprise, they just could not do it.

6 Jewish Leaders Stand Firm against Jesus (7:45–52)

The temple guards came back without their prisoner. The Jewish leaders were furious and demanded an explanation. Verse 46—"No one ever spoke the way this man does," they answered.

More and more people were taking Jesus seriously. Now even the temple guards were on His side. That was too much for the Jewish leaders. They lashed out at the guards. "You too?" they complained. "Why do you listen to Him and to the mob? Why don't you listen to us? We're the experts, and we condemn Him as a fraud."

One of the Jewish leaders, Nicodemus, who had visited with Jesus on a previous occasion (chapter 3) objected. "This man has never had a hearing before us. We can't condemn someone without a hearing. That would be illegal."

The others snapped back. "Are you from Galilee, too, as He is? Is that why you speak up for Him? Don't you know that prophets do not come from Galilee?" That was neither correct nor the answer to his question. It was an expression of their great anger and frustration. Despite everything they said and did, more and more people were accepting Jesus.

7 Jesus Addresses the Case of a Woman Caught in Adultery (7:53–8:11)

This section almost certainly was not originally part of John's Gospel. It may be an accurate report of things that Jesus did and said, inserted here to preserve it.

The case against this woman seemed to offer her no defense. She had been caught in the act, apprehended, and summarily brought to Jesus. The law prescribed that she be stoned.

In fact, the law said that both she and her partner be stoned to death. This brings up a question: Where was her partner in the sin in which she had been caught? Had he successfully escaped? If they had been caught in the act of adultery, that hardly seems likely. More likely the fact that only the woman was brought to Jesus betrays a prejudice held by the Pharisees against women. Such a prejudice would fit in with their smug attitudes.

And why did they bring the woman to Jesus? They needed no advice about what should be done with her. No, this amounted to another attempt to trap Jesus, to place Him in a position where He must either be merciless or in defiance of the law.

Jesus handles the situation in a masterful way. He upholds the law but turns its harsh spotlight back on the woman's accusers. He invites the accuser who is himself without sin to throw the first stone against her. While He waits for that man to step forward, Jesus bends down to write in the dust. To write what? We can only guess. But, in any case, the woman's accusers melt away in the hot glare of the very same law they had turned upon her.

Jesus does not excuse the woman. He calls on her to repent, extending to her God's forgiving grace and the power to leave her sin behind. Jesus' words to the guilty woman offer grace and help to all of us when the glare of God's Law is turned upon us and exposes our own sins against God.

8 Jesus Defends His Testimony (8:12–30)

While the chief priests and some Pharisees were interrogating the guards, other Pharisees were in the temple carrying on a debate with Jesus. He gave them something startling to deal with. Verse 12—"I am the light of the world. Whoever follows Me will never walk in darkness, but will have the light of life." They objected that He was testifying about Himself. Jesus responded by saying that didn't matter, because He knew what He was talking about. Besides, the Father confirmed His testimony. But, since they didn't know His Father, they probably would not accept His testimony either.

At this point, Jesus sensed a complete breakdown of communication. No matter what He said, they would not believe. He issued a warning. He was going to leave them and, unless they believed, they would die in their sins. He came from the Father to deliver His message, to be His message. The consequences of rejecting Him are fatal. When they finally would have their way with Him and nail Him to a cross, they would realize what a mistake they had made.

Verse 30—Although the Pharisees would not change their minds, many others who heard Jesus say these things did believe.

Concluding Activities

Close this session by asking participants to think silently for a moment about how they might have been unresponsive to God's desire to communicate with them through His Word. Then speak a prayer asking God's forgiveness for our failures to receive God's communication to us through His Word. Ask the Holy Spirit's help in making us more responsive to the Word of God and more eager to hear it.

Make any necessary announcements and distribute study leaflet 7.

Notes

Notes

Communication Breakthrough

John 8:31–9:41

Preparing for the Session

Central Focus

By miraculously restoring sight to a blind man, Jesus prepared him for an even greater miracle—faith—but further alienated His enemies.

Objectives

That participants, by the power of the Holy Spirit working through the Word,

1. joyously take advantage of the communication opportunities Jesus provides;

2. accept their disabilities and limitations as opportunities for God to do something special in their lives;

3. acknowledge that their personal faith is a miracle of spiritual healing and not their own doing;

4. repent of their inclinations to unbelief.

Note for small-group leaders: Lesson notes and other materials you will need begin on page 82.

For the Lecture Leader

What you are like when you are not in front of the group can help or hinder your presentations tremendously. What you say, how you act, how you relate to people outside of class affects the way people respond to what you present in class.

Obviously, there is a clear warning in this. Don't impair your effectiveness by being insincere, insensitive, or unfriendly. Someone once said to a preacher, "What you are speaks so loudly that I can't hear what you are saying."

The positive side is that you don't have to be a great scholar or speaker in order to be an effective presenter. If you build and sustain good relationships with your learners, if they discover that you are genuinely interested in them, that you personally believe and live by what you are presenting, if they have learned to respect you—then they will listen to you and benefit from what you present. An important part of your preparation as a presenter takes place apart from your study time. It takes place over coffee, in heart-to-heart personal conversations, in gestures of consideration and kindness.

Don't neglect study and delivery. They are essential. But be sure also to give adequate attention to impressions that you create outside of class and to relationships that you have with people in other settings.

God's Word is communicated most effectively through close personal relationships. Every presenter of God's Word needs to work as creatively and faithfully at this aspect of the presentation as at study and delivery.

Session Plan

Worship

Begin the session with the hymn and prayer printed in the study leaflet. Accompaniments are available in denominational hymnals, such as *Lutheran Worship* (refer to hymnal index), or on the *Every Voice a Song* CD set.

Lecture Presentation

1 Were Those Who Opposed Jesus Children of Abraham or Children of the Devil (8:31–47)?

Verse 31—Others, however, who previously had believed, now no longer believed. Jesus turned to them and said, "You are My followers only if you hold on to My teaching. If you do that you will know the truth, and the truth will set you free."

"We're already free," they insisted. "We always have been, because we're descendants of Abraham."

"You may be children of Abraham," Jesus replied, "but you are also slaves to sin. Your determination to kill Me proves that. You didn't learn that from Abraham. You have another father besides him."

"God is our true Father," they claimed.

"If He were, you would love Me and listen to Me, because I came from Him and speak for Him. No, your father is the devil. He has been a liar and murderer from the beginning. Obviously, he is the one you are hearing and following."

2 Jesus Makes the Ultimate Claim (8:48–59)

"You're the one who is demon possessed," they argued. "You misrepresent God, like the Samaritans do."

"No," Jesus insisted, "I am simply honoring God by saying and doing what He wants Me to. You ought to listen to Me. A lot is at stake. Whoever accepts and holds on to what I say will never die."

"You go too far," they complained. "The greatest of God's people died, even Abraham and the prophets. Are You greater than they?"

"Your father Abraham was delighted to know about Me and what I am doing," Jesus responded.

"How can this be?" they asked. "You aren't even 50 years old. How could you and Abraham know each other?"

"I'm serious," Jesus said. "Even before Abraham was, I am."

They were outraged. "I AM" was a name that God gave Himself (Exodus 3:14). To their way of thinking, this made Jesus a blasphemer, who ought to be executed by stoning. But when they tried to do this, they couldn't. Jesus slipped away. His time had not yet come.

3 Jesus Responds to Communication Breakdown

How do you suppose Jesus feels when people spoil His attempts to communicate with them and to relate to them? How do you suppose He feels toward us when we don't listen to Him or take Him at His word? We may not reject Him as many of these people did. We may simply ignore Him or tune out His Word when it is directed toward us. How does He feel about this kind of communication breakdown?

In view of this, we need to admit our guilt for causing the communication breakdown. This is no small matter.

Nevertheless, we may accept His pardon gratefully and confidently. He means it when He says He paid for all of our sins on the cross. We can take Him at His Word about this.

And we can eagerly take advantage of the communication opportunities He so generously provides. Conversation with God is a high privilege. How amazing that He wants to speak to us through His Word! How astonishing that He is willing to listen to our prayers! The communication lines are open for us. Let's get the conversation going and keep it going.

4 Jesus Confronts Two Kinds of Blindness

In chapter 9 Jesus confronts two kinds of blindness. A man had been blind since the day he was born. He had never seen the friendly, smiling face of a loved one. He had never seen flowers blooming in the warm sunshine of a spring day. He had never seen anything. Can you imagine what that would be like?

In addition, this man and others in the story suffered from spiritual blindness. They did not know and believe in their Savior. They had no faith.

Jesus performed two miracles. He restored this man's vision and brought him to faith. Two miracles—the second one was the greater.

5 Who Sinned? Are Disabilities Punishment (9:1–5)?

When they came upon a blind man begging by the side of the road, the disciples couldn't help but wonder: Why would God permit someone to go through life with such a handicap?

At the time when Jesus walked this earth, many Jews assumed that such disabilities were a consequence of personal sin. When they asked Jesus about this, He explained emphatically that God had a different reason in this case. This man's blindness was not a consequence of a specific sin on his part. Rather, it was an opportunity for God to do something very special.

This speaks to us. We, too, have disabilities and limitations. As we struggle with these things, we often feel abused by God or deprived. From what Jesus said and did here, we get a new perspective. Disabilities are never punishment to the Christian. They are opportunities.

God may let them happen to us only because He wants to do something special to us through them. He may correct them, or He may strengthen us to endure them. In any case, He promises to make them a blessing for us.

Jesus described what He was going to do in interesting terms. "I won't be around much longer. But, while I'm here, I am going to bring God's light into this dark world." In 1 John 1:5 John tells us that God is light. Here Jesus says that He is the light of the world. That means that Jesus is God come into the world to make Himself known. If we want to know what God is like, if we want to see His goodness, His compassion, His power, all we need to do is watch Jesus. In Jesus, God is present and active in a way that people can see and relate to.

Darkness is everything that's wrong with us and our world. Suffering, disability, sin, unbelief, death—all are the work of God's enemy, the devil—the prince of darkness. They are ways in which he torments us and tries to destroy us forever.

Jesus came to undo, to reverse the work of darkness. This man's blindness kept him from experiencing some of the beauty of this world. Jesus was going to drive away the darkness that surrounded him—both the physical and the spiritual darkness.

6 Jesus Restores the Blind Man's Vision (9:6–12)

With saliva and dirt, Jesus made some mud and applied it to the man's eyes. He told him to wash in the Pool of Siloam. The man must have wondered what this was all about. Jesus had not really explained. He had only said that God's work would be displayed in him. But what did that mean?

In any case, the blind man was grateful for the unusual interest. He appreciated that Jesus said his blindness was not a consequence of his sin. So he was ready to do what Jesus instructed. He found his way to the pool, then washed the mud from his eyes, and, to his amazement, he discovered that he could see.

People who knew him were astonished. Isn't this the blind man who used to sit here and beg? Some said, "Of course it is." Others said, "It couldn't be. It only looks like him." The man who had been blind settled the argument. "I'm the one," he said. "How in the world did you gain your sight?" they asked him. He explained what Jesus had said and done. "Where is Jesus?" they inquired. "I really don't know," he answered.

This is not the first blind person whom Jesus healed. Six others are mentioned in other Gospels (Matthew 9:27–31; 12:22; 20:29–34; Mark 8:22–26). However, this is the only case in which He healed a person who is said to have been born blind. Healing the blind was an act of compassion toward people with an especially tragic disability. But there is even more to it than that. It also marked Jesus as the Christ, the promised Savior. In three different places (29:18; 35:5; 42:7) the prophet Isaiah described the Christ as the One who would give sight to the blind.

7 The Pharisees Investigate (9:13–23)

The neighbors and acquaintances of the man who had been blind brought him to the Pharisees. The reason for this is not given. The Pharisees were a highly respected group among the Jews. They were regarded as being very serious about their religion and knowledgeable. Perhaps those who brought the man simply wanted their opinion about the matter. They may have remembered the prophecies of Isaiah and wondered if this meant that Jesus was the Christ. Or, because this healing was performed on the Sabbath, they may have been concerned about a possible violation.

The Pharisees were interested in the remarkable cure. On an earlier occasion (5:1–9), Jesus had angered them by healing the invalid at Bethesda on the Sabbath. Now He had done it again. They were going to have to deal more decisively with Him.

The Pharisees asked the man who had been blind to explain what happened. Some of them immediately condemned Jesus. They were sure that He was not from God because He had not kept the Sabbath as they interpreted it. Others were more positive. "Could someone who was disobeying God perform such a miracle?" they asked. As in the events described in the previous lesson, many rejected Him, but there were also some with whom there was a communication breakthrough. In what Jesus said and did, they recognized God's own message.

Verse 17—The Pharisees asked the man who had been

healed his opinion about Jesus. Even though these powerful religious leaders had condemned Jesus, this man dared to pay Him the highest tribute he could think of. "He is a prophet," the man replied. He put Jesus in a class with Moses and Elijah and others through whom God had performed miracles of healing. Of course, this is still less than the full truth. But the man's impression of Jesus was developing significantly. Verse 11—In his first reference to Jesus, he simply described Him as "the man they call Jesus." Now he calls Him a prophet.

Disgusted with what the investigation was turning up, the Pharisees dismissed the man and called his parents before them. They were still not convinced that the man had been born blind. His parents could settle that question and, perhaps, explain the alleged healing in a way that was more to their liking.

The parents were cautious. They knew that the leaders were out to get anyone who in any way suggested that Jesus was the Christ. Such people were to be expelled from the synagogue. Since the synagogue was the center of life in any Jewish community (particularly outside of Jerusalem itself), expulsion from the synagogue would be a severe penalty, with social and economic repercussions. However, they did present the basic facts. "He is our son. He was born blind. Now he sees. But we don't know how this happened. Ask him. He is an adult and can speak for himself."

8　They Expel the Man Who Had Been Healed (9:24–34)

Once again they summoned the man who had been healed. They pressed him hard. "Tell the truth. Give God the credit for what happened to you, not Jesus. This man is a sinner. He breaks the Sabbath."

But the man stuck to the facts. "I don't know whether or not He is a sinner," the man explained. "But I do know this. Once I was blind and now I see."

The Pharisees wanted more information about the process through which his sight was restored. "Tell us again what happened," they demanded. "How did He do it?"

At this, the man became assertive, even sarcastic. "What is this?" he asked. "How many times do I have to tell you? You are really fascinated by this, aren't you? Maybe you would like to be His disciples too."

This really provoked them. "You're the one who is His disciple. We're disciples of Moses. God really spoke to him. But this Jesus in an unknown. We don't even know where He came from."

"You people are unbelievable," the formerly blind man said. "A man does a great miracle—something that no one else ever did. You don't know anything about Him, but you're sure that He's a sinner. Here is something we all know: God doesn't cooperate this way with sinners. If He were not from God, Jesus could not possibly have done this."

"How dare you talk to us like this!" they replied. "You're the sinner—from your very birth. Otherwise you wouldn't have been born blind. For your reckless and blasphemous words you are excommunicated from the synagogue."

9　Jesus Makes a Communication Breakthrough (9:35–41)

By word and deed Jesus was trying to get through to this man with the full saving truth about Himself. As we have noted, the man's understanding of and commitment to Jesus were developing. But they were not complete. In this final episode, Jesus makes a communication breakthrough and brings the man to saving faith.

After his final encounter with the Pharisees, the man who had been healed went off by himself. He was probably stunned by the severity of the penalty. He may have been somewhat surprised at his bold statements to them. Perhaps for the first time he had an opportunity to reflect on the amazing events.

When Jesus heard what had happened to the man, He looked until He found him. The man had lost his synagogue privileges. Jesus was going to offer him something far better in its place.

Verse 35—"Do you believe in the Son of Man?" Jesus asked him. In his reply, we can sense the man's growing respect and appreciation for Jesus. The more he thought about Jesus and what He had done, the more confidence he had in Him. With His question Jesus seemed to be recommending faith in someone called "the Son of Man." This man wasn't quite sure who the Son of Man was, but if Jesus wanted him to believe in Him, he would be more than happy to do this. "Just tell me who He is, Lord, and I will believe in Him."

Jesus answered, "You are looking at the Son of Man, My friend, and listening to Him." With that there was an exciting communication breakthrough. Things came together in the man's mind. Perhaps Jesus made some additional comments—that He was God's Son sent from heaven to make God known and to make sinners right with God by His suffering and death. However it happened, Jesus communicated clearly to the man about Himself, and the man understood and accepted.

He called Jesus Lord, believed in Him, and worshiped Him. What a miracle! Whenever anyone believes, God has performed a miracle. He has opened their eyes of faith. As we think of our personal faith, we need to be aware of this. Faith may seem to be something we do— we hear or read; we understand; we want Him; we trust in Him. But, in fact, we are able to do this only because the power of the Holy Spirit has enabled us to believe.

Probably a little bit later Jesus met up with the Pharisees again. The man may have been with Him. "Something strange has happened here today," Jesus observed. "A man who was blind both physically and spiritually now can see in both ways. Yet others, who are very sure of themselves and the clarity of their vision, are, in fact, blind."

The Pharisees realized they were the ones to whom Jesus was referring. "Are You saying that we are blind?" they asked. "If you realized you were blind, there would be hope for you," Jesus answered. "But since you insist that you can see, you have to accept responsibility for what you are doing in rejecting Me."

We shake our heads at the Pharisees and their negative response to Jesus. They refused to listen to Him. They were determined to reject Him.

Something in us reacts in much the same way, though perhaps more subtly. Even though we believe and trust in Jesus, the forces of spiritual darkness and unbelief are active in us. We may not reject Him outright as the Pharisees did. However, we may push Him into the background of our lives. We often ignore Him or are easily distracted from Him. We find ourselves living and making our decisions with very little awareness of Him. Our spiritual vision, too, needs His healing touch.

On another occasion (Mark 9:24), a man whom Jesus challenged to believe more confidently said, "I do believe; help me overcome my unbelief." Faith and unbelief exist side by side in all of us. We need to respond the way this man did. We affirm our faith and confess our unbelief.

In 1 John 1:8–9 John says all this beautifully. "If we claim to be without sin, we deceive ourselves and the truth is not in us. If we confess our sins, He is faithful and just and will forgive us our sins and purify us from all unrighteousness."

Concluding Activities

As you close this session, give participants an opportunity to express their faith by reading or reciting the Apostles' Creed together. Since everyone may not know this creed by heart, provide copies for everyone.

Make any necessary announcements and distribute study leaflet 8.

Notes

Notes

Communication at Its Best

John 10:1–42

Preparing for the Session

Central Focus

Jesus describes the close, caring, saving relationship He has with those who hear and accept Him.

Objectives

That participants, by the power of the Holy Spirit working through the Word,

1. recognize as true spiritual leaders only those who lead others to God and His people through Jesus;

2. listen eagerly to the voice of Jesus in Word and Sacrament;

3. experience closeness and security in their relationship to Him as their God and Savior.

Note for small-group leaders: Lesson notes and other materials you will need begin on page 85.

For the Lecture Leader

A vital step in preparing to share God's Word with others is to ponder it thoughtfully for yourself. What is the Good Shepherd saying to you in this marvelous 10th chapter? How is He trying to deepen your relationship with Him? How is He trying to improve your communication with Him?

Do you recognize yourself as presenter anywhere in this chapter? As a teacher of God's Word, you are an undershepherd, one who leads a group of God's sheep to feed on the pastures of His Word, and who then leads them back again into the safety of the fold.

The way to be a faithful undershepherd is to do what you do through Jesus Christ, the chief shepherd and watchman of the flock. Approach your group of hearers trusting in Jesus to be with you. Make Jesus Himself the heart and center of all your teaching. Stand before His flock as His servant and witness.

Meditate deeply on the sacrificial love of the Good Shepherd for you. That is the climax of His ministry. Consider how desperately you need His atoning death. Rejoice in His willingness to do all this for you.

Remember that as an undershepherd you are also one of His sheep. Listen carefully for His voice, His warm and comforting words of pardon and hope. Look forward eagerly to the eternal life He promises you.

These are just a few specific and personal words that your Lord wants to say to you through this chapter. There are many more. There is no better way to prepare to share Him with others than to listen attentively to Him yourself.

Session Plan

Worship

Begin the session with the hymn and prayer printed in the study leaflet. Accompaniments are available in denominational hymnals, such as *Lutheran Worship* (refer to hymnal index), or on the *Every Voice a Song* CD set.

Lecture Presentation

1 Jesus Speaks about a Shepherd and His Sheep (10:1–6)

The relationship between Jesus and His followers is a lot like that between a shepherd and his sheep. It is a beautiful relationship—close, caring, trusting—a relationship that fosters communication at its best.

To understand and appreciate what Jesus is saying in this chapter, it helps to know something about how sheep were cared for in Jesus' day. Even now in that part of the world, care of sheep is done in much the same way. It is very different from the way it is done in our part of the world. From Jesus' words here and from what the Bible says elsewhere, we know quite a bit about their way of caring for sheep. In what follows we will try to give a clear picture. However, some of the details are somewhat uncertain.

The arrangement that Jesus describes here appears to be one in which there are a chief shepherd and several under shepherds. The chief shepherd owns and manages a large, walled enclosure called a sheep pen. In this he keeps his sheep at night to protect them from thieves and robbers. The enclosure also keeps the sheep from wandering and protects them from wild animals.

In addition to his own sheep, those of several other shepherds are kept in his pen at night. These are men with smaller flocks, who cannot afford their own pen. The chief shepherd controls the door to the sheep pen. He is the watchman. At night only those shepherds whom he recognizes may bring their sheep into the pen. Early in the morning only those men whose sheep are in the pen can go inside and get them and lead them out to pasture. The chief shepherd carefully guards the door against intruders. Anyone who is not permitted to come through the gate and who instead tries to go over the wall is up to no good. He is not a shepherd. He is a thief and a robber.

The shepherd Jesus describes in John 10:1–6 does not have a huge flock with thousands of sheep—only a few dozen, or, at most, a hundred. He knows each sheep and calls it by name. They are more like pets or children than range livestock. They recognize his voice and respond to it. When he calls, they come. They follow their shepherd and no one else. They have learned to trust him.

Their trust is not misplaced. Their shepherd provides for them. He leads them to choice pastures and cool, sweet water. He guards them against danger. He goes after them when they stray. He protects them against wolves and other predators. When danger comes, he does not run away. These sheep are his. They depend on him. He risks his life and may even lose it—in order to save his sheep.

2 Jesus Is the Gate for the Sheep (10:7–10)

Jesus addresses these beautiful words to the Pharisees. This chapter continues His conversation with them after the healing of the blind man. Remember several impor-

tant things about these Pharisees: (1) They regarded themselves as spiritual leaders of God's people. They were very serious and knowledgeable about their religion. They were deeply committed to living by God's will—as they understood it. Most of their fellow Jews looked to them for spiritual leadership. (2) Most were out to get Jesus. They were convinced that He was a fraud, that He ought to be killed because He claimed to be Lord of the Sabbath. (3) Some were reacting more positively. They were beginning to think that maybe He was the Christ after all.

To this divided group of Pharisees Jesus speaks of sheep and shepherds. These men who claimed to be spiritual leaders of God's people hear from Jesus what it means and what it takes to be such leaders. Spiritual leaders are the shepherds of God's flock. This was taught in the Old Testament. (See Ezekiel 34, for example.) The only way to enter God's flock, either as a shepherd or a sheep, is through the gate. And Jesus says that He is that gate. Only those who approach God and His people through Jesus will enter the safety of His flock. Others are dangerous intruders.

Through this figure of speech, Jesus is making an astonishing claim: If you want to belong to God, if you want to lead God's people, you have to do it through Me. If you do enter God's flock through faith in Me, you will be well taken care of. I have life in its fullness for you. If you try to lead God's people without accepting and obeying Me, you will only hurt and deprive God's flock. And, you will lose salvation too. What will you be—a true shepherd of the sheep or a thief and a robber?

Many in every age, including our own, present themselves as God's representatives and spokespersons, as leaders of His people. Here Jesus gives us a reliable gauge by which to evaluate them. True shepherds lead others to God and His flock through Jesus. They themselves know and trust in Jesus as their Savior. And they invite and encourage others to find their way to God through Him. No one who ignores or denies Jesus can be trusted or followed.

3 Jesus Is the Good Shepherd (10:11–21)

When He refers to Himself as the Good Shepherd, Jesus calls attention to His supreme sacrifice on behalf of His sheep. Verse 11—"The good shepherd lays down his life for the sheep." If the one watching the sheep is only a hired person, he will run away when danger comes. He cares more about himself than he does about the sheep. The good shepherd, who truly cares for the sheep, faces the danger on their behalf and dies in order to save them.

Jesus describes a beautiful bond and a wonderful relationship between the Good Shepherd and the sheep, between Jesus and His followers. He says they know each other just as the heavenly Father and His Son know each other. They know each other as only those who truly love each other can. Jesus loves those who are already His sheep. And He loves and wants those who still need to be brought into His flock.

As He moves toward His sacrificial, atoning death for people, the Good Shepherd makes it clear that He is not a tragic victim of death. Rather, He is the confident master of death and will become the victor over it.

These words are an urgent invitation to all who hear or read them. They were originally addressed to the Pharisees. Most of them were stubbornly opposed to Him. Others were on the brink of faith. He invites and urges them to accept Him. "I love you so much that I will die for you. I am the Good Shepherd and the Savior that you need."

He also directs these words to us. "Remember who your shepherd is," He is pleading in this passage. "Remember that He laid down His life for you. I am a shepherd whom you can love and trust. I am your Good Shepherd."

The reaction of His enemies, the Pharisees, here called "the Jews," was again divided. Many said that He was demon possessed, mad, not fit to listen to. Others, reflecting on His words and on His miraculous cure of the blind man, said that this was not the work of a demoniac.

4 Jesus Makes a Final Attempt to Win His Enemies Over (10:22–33)

Some of Jesus' most beautiful and winsome words were addressed to His enemies. Although most Pharisees and the other Jewish leaders were becoming increasingly hard and bitter in their opposition to Him, Jesus kept trying to win them over.

He did not mince words with them. He sharply denounced their unbelief. Nor did He weaken His high claims about Himself—claims to which they vehemently objected. But He also tried to draw them toward Himself with an appealing description of what it's like to believe in Him and belong to Him. And He tried to convince them from Scripture that His claims were valid.

Although this discussion picks up the shepherd theme again, it occurs sometime after the incident described in the first part of this chapter. It took place during the Feast of Dedication, or Hanukkah. His enemies gathered around Jesus in the temple. They demanded a simple, straightforward answer to the question: Are you the Christ?

Many of the things that Jesus had said and done pointed unmistakably to a yes. However, He had never said to them, "Yes, I am the Christ." Now He tells them, "My miracles are your answer. You are aware of them. But you don't believe. That is, you don't accept Me for what these works show Me to be—the Christ, your promised Savior. You're not My sheep. That is really too bad. Wouldn't you like to be My sheep, My followers? I don't have any difficulty communicating with My sheep. They listen to Me, and I listen to them. I know them, and they come to Me. And do you know where I lead them? To eternal life. Our relationship will never be broken, not even by death."

In these words we Christians find a most appealing description of our relationship with our Lord and our communication with Him. He is always with us—protecting, providing, and leading the way. Through His Word He constantly reassures us. His open heart is always ready to receive our petitions and our praise. Our opportunity to communicate with Him never ends, and it's communication at its best!

And implied in all of this is a beautiful invitation to the Pharisees and to anyone else who hears it. "Quit fighting Me. Believe. Be My sheep."

And then He said something that made them explode with anger. Verse 30—He said, "I and the Father are one." This is the clearest statement of His deity that He ever made to them. On an earlier occasion (5:16–18) Jesus infuriated them with a similar, but less direct, comment. He said that because He was God's Son, it was all right for Him to work on the Sabbath. They correctly understood that by calling God His Father, He was making Himself equal with God. Verse 31—Now He said something even more emphatic, "I and the Father are one."

"He claims to be God. He insults God. He must die." And they prepared to kill Him with stones.

Jesus reacted with incredible calmness. "Why are you doing this?" He inquired. "I did many miracles at My Father's direction and with His power. Which one of these makes you want to do this to Me?"

"It's not the miracles," they snarled. "It's what You said. You're only a man, but You claim to be God. That's blasphemy."

5 Jesus Appeals to Scripture (10:34–39)

To try to calm them down, Jesus called their attention to a remarkable passage in the psalms (Psalm 82:6). "Why do you get so upset because I refer to myself as the Son of God? In the Scriptures, rulers and judges are referred to as 'gods.' If it's all right to do that, why is it wrong for Me to call Myself the 'Son of God'? After all, the Father set Me apart in a special way and sent Me into the world."

"Judge Me by what I do. Am I not doing Godlike things?"

To the very end of this last debate with His enemies, Jesus is trying to put a hole in their wall of resistance. But their anger and opposition were adamant. They moved in to capture Him. But once again He evaded them.

6 New Sheep Enter the Fold (10:40–42)

Following this painful confrontation with the Pharisees, Jesus left Jerusalem. He went across the Jordan where He had first met John the Baptist and had been baptized by Him (chapter 1). Once again people came to Him in large numbers. Their interest had been awakened by John's preaching. They discovered that Jesus was all that John said He was. They believed in Him, and, in believing, they became sheep of His flock.

They heard His voice and followed Him. He heard their prayers and answered them. They experienced real communication—communication at its best.

Concluding Activities

Close by turning again to the opening hymn, which paraphrases Psalm 23. This time have participants hum the hymn softly while one person (you or someone you appoint) reads the words.

Then make any necessary announcements and distribute study leaflet 9.

Notes

Ultimate Purpose: Death-Transcending Relationships

John 11:1–57

Preparing for the Session

Central Focus

By raising His dead friend to life, Jesus points to what He will accomplish through His own death and resurrection—a relationship with His followers that extends beyond death.

Objectives

That participants, by the power of the Holy Spirit working through the Word,

1. bring their needs to Jesus;

2. face death with the sure hope of life eternal through Jesus' death and resurrection;

3. find comfort in the fact that their relationships with Him and believing loved ones will never end;

4. accept delay as a sign of His love;

5. recognize the death and resurrection of Lazarus as a prelude to Jesus' death and resurrection and all that they will accomplish.

Note for small-group leaders: Lesson notes and other materials you will need begin on page 88.

For the Lecture Leader

Our lesson today is a true story. It is an account of some things that happened. An important part of being a presenter is being an effective storyteller. You must also explain some of the meaning of the story. But first, the story itself must get through to your hearers.

Telling a story well is an art. But it is also something that can be learned, at least in part. Effective storytellers know there are many keys to good storytelling, including this one: You must enter the thoughts and feelings of the characters and then draw your listeners with you.

As you study this 11th chapter of John's Gospel, reflect on the thoughts and feelings of all concerned.

For example, what did Mary and Martha think and feel when

- their brother became deathly sick?
- Jesus was so slow in getting there?
- so many friends came to console them?
- Jesus broke down and cried with them?
- He wanted to open the tomb?
- their brother walked out of the tomb?

What did Jesus think and feel when

- His disciples discouraged Him from returning to the area near Jerusalem?
- Thomas spoke up as He did?
- the sisters complained about His being late?
- everyone was weeping at the tomb?
- Lazarus came back from death at His command?

Also consider the thoughts and feelings of Jesus' enemies as they plotted His death.

In other words, try to get inside these people. Much of what you come up with may be speculation. But, unless it contradicts what the Bible says, it may be helpful. It may make the story more real and meaningful to you. As a result, you will be able to make it more real and meaningful to your hearers.

Session Plan

Worship

Begin the session with the hymn and prayer printed in the study leaflet. Accompaniments are available in denominational hymnals, such as *Lutheran Worship* (refer to hymnal index) or on the *Every Voice a Song* CD set.

Lecture Presentation

1 They Brought Their Needs to Jesus (11:1–3)

With divine power and love Jesus met many needs. In chapter 11 Jesus is confronted with a need even more serious than before. He is brought face-to-face with death itself. What adds to the intensity and drama of the situation is that the person overtaken by death is His good friend Lazarus.

The sisters were frantic when Lazarus took a turn for the worse. They realized that unless something could be done, he would not live much longer. The prospect of losing their brother was painful and frightening. Besides that, who would provide for them if he were gone? In their fear and sorrow over Lazarus's serious illness, they did the right thing. Verse 3—They brought their need to Jesus.

That is something for us to think about carefully. We too have urgent and frightening needs. It may be sickness and the threat of death, such as these people faced. It may be the loss of a job or a troubled marriage. It may be loneliness. You know what your needs are, and I know what mine are. Often our needs dominate our lives and threaten to overwhelm us. No matter what we are doing, these needs claim our attention and disturb us.

How do we deal with these needs? What do we do about them? Often we dwell on them; we cringe before them. In our desperation we may go from one person to another. We tell our story and look for some encouragement and relief. We may try all kinds of questionable helpers. Or we may give up and sink into depression. When our needs are great and pressing, we often handle them badly, if we deal with them at all.

The way that Mary and Martha took was far, far better. They brought their need to Jesus. Notice how they expressed themselves. They didn't specify the solution. They didn't tell Him how to address the need. They simply told Him about it.

Bring *your* needs to Jesus. He already knows about them, of course. But He wants you to bring them to Him anyway. It's good for you to face the need squarely and ask for His help. Then when help comes it will mean all the more to you. Just present the need. That's enough. If you want to request the specific help that you want, that's fine too. But the most important thing is that you, like Mary and Martha, bring your need to Jesus.

2 Jesus Makes a Loving Delay (11:4–16)

Jesus' response is significant. In the first place, He expresses complete understanding of the condition, including its outcome. The sickness will not end in death. (However, as we will see, it did lead to death.) But the main reason for the sickness is that God and His Son might be glorified.

Then comes a surprise. Jesus loved Lazarus. And yet He waited two days before going to see him. That doesn't sound like love, does it? We often interpret a delay as a lack of interest on the Lord's part. But here we learn that there is such a thing as a loving delay. Our Lord has a wonderful sense of timing. Because He loves us so much, He waits with His help until we will get maximum benefit from it.

The disciples were not surprised when Jesus stayed where He was. The authorities in Jerusalem were after His life. Why should He walk into their trap? Verse 7— What surprised them was when Jesus announced that He was going to go to Lazarus near Jerusalem after all.

Verse 14—Jesus then explained that Lazarus had fallen asleep, meaning the sleep of death. They thought He meant natural sleep. In that case, they said, the crisis is past, and he will be all right. Jesus clarified, "No, he is dead, but I'm glad, because this is going to do your faith a lot of good. Let's go."

Apparently the disciples hesitated. They wondered if it was safe for them to accompany Him. After all, if His enemies took Jesus, they might also go after His followers. While they stalled for time to consider this, one of them called the others to action. In words expressing great courage and loyalty, he challenged them to set aside their fears (v. 16), "Let us also go, that we may die with Him."

Who made this heroic statement? Someone you would least expect. It was Thomas, called Didymus, which means "twin." We usually refer to him as "doubting Thomas," because later on (20:24–40) he did not believe that the risen Lord had appeared to the other disciples. However, at this point, Thomas is full of courageous faith. He said what none of the others dared to say, "Let us also go, that we may die with Him."

3 Jesus Brings Hope to Mourners (11:17–37)

Finally, two days later than expected, Jesus arrived at Bethany where His grieving friends lived. Many of their other friends, including a large number from nearby Jerusalem, were there paying their respects and extending their sympathy. All of us can appreciate how much that meant to these women who had lost their brother.

But when Martha heard that Jesus was near, she realized that He could provide help and hope that no one else could offer. She hurried out to meet Him. Before He could say anything, she expressed her disappointment in His delay, saying that if He had come sooner, Lazarus would not have died. But she quickly added a statement of beautiful confidence in Him. She knew that even now, it was not too late. She knew that God could and would do anything that Jesus asked.

Jesus spoke directly to her confidence. Verse 23—"Your brother will rise again." Martha agreed that Lazarus would rise on the Last Day. What she said also implied that she was hoping for something even before that great day of resurrection.

In reply, Jesus offered spectacular, powerful hope in the face of death. This was for Martha and Mary. It is also for everyone else who believes in Him. Jesus brings this hope to us. When death is staring us in the face, when we are mourning the loss of a loved one, Jesus assures us that He can and will do something about that death.

Jesus is the resurrection and the life. He will personally experience death and resurrection. He will die the death that we have earned by our sins. He will come back from death again to show that our sins have been paid for. He will rise from death to show us that He has made a way for us through death to a life that never ends. Those who trust in Him, who by that faith are in a saving, personal relationship with Him, will continue in that relationship even after death strikes. Those who live and believe in Him will never die.

That means that all those who live and die in faith have relationships with one another that last beyond death. When we meet our Lord on the other side of death, we will also be reunited with all of our Christian loved ones. Those who have died ahead of us will be there to greet us and welcome us into glory.

What incomparable hope and comfort in the face of death! To Martha all this was a promise. It was going to happen in the near future. For us Jesus' death and resurrection are accomplished facts.

When He brings hope to those who need it, Jesus expects a response of faith. He expected it from Martha, and He expects it from us. He expects faith, because with the offer of hope He also provides us with the power to believe. His Spirit accompanies the offer and enables us to believe. "Do you believe this?" He asked Martha after He offered to be her resurrection and life. Martha's reply was superb. It was as fine a confession of faith as anyone could make (v. 27): "Yes, Lord . . . I believe that You are the Christ, the Son of God, who was to come into the world." Jesus addresses the same question to us. We can do no better than to make Martha's confession our own.

Martha and Jesus were soon joined by Mary. As she ran to find Jesus just outside the village, many of her friends came along. Verse 32—When Mary met Jesus she said exactly what Martha had said to Him earlier: "Lord, if You had been here, my brother would not have died." Then she broke down, sobbing uncontrollably. Her friends wept with her. Jesus was touched by their sorrow and their weeping. "Where is the tomb?" He asked them. "We'll show you," they answered.

Then Jesus, too, broke into tears. (The Greek word denotes quiet weeping.) He loved these grieving people and knew how they felt. Even though He was about to meet their need in a decisive way, His emotions were responding to their present grief. When He wept openly and unashamedly, some of those present recognized that His weeping grew out of His love for Lazarus. Others wondered if Jesus could have prevented this tragic death. If He loved Lazarus, why didn't He heal him as He healed the blind man?

The next time you weep at the grave of a loved one or friend, remember that tears can be an appropriate and healthy reaction. Jesus Himself cried. Even though you know that the person's soul is with the Lord now and that the body will be raised at the Last Day, you and others are separated from that loved one for a time, and that hurts. In addition, remember that Jesus understands how you feel. Believe in Him. Lean on Him. He will comfort you and eventually turn your sorrow into joy.

4 He Raises the Dead (11:38–44)

Still trembling with emotion, Jesus approached the tomb, which was a cave with a stone covering the entrance. What happened next was by far the most spectacular miracle that Jesus ever performed. He ordered them to remove the stone. The sisters objected that the corpse, now four days old, would smell of decay. Jesus insisted, and the stone was removed. Then He prayed aloud to the Father for the benefit of all who were present, that they might believe—that is, that they might recognize and accept Him as their God and Savior through what was to happen.

When His prayer to the Father ended, Jesus raised His voice and gave a bold command to the corpse. Verse 43—"Lazarus, come out!" And, incredibly, Lazarus did. Still wrapped in grave clothes, with no smell of death about him, Lazarus walked out of what was supposed to be his final resting place. Jesus had released him from death—a man who had been in the grave for four days! But he was still bound by his burial garments. Verse 44—"Take off the grave clothes and let him go," Jesus said.

The death and resurrection of Lazarus was a prelude to Jesus' own death and resurrection. In less than two weeks Jesus would experience something far more dreadful than the death that Lazarus went through. And He would come crashing out of death again in an even more glorious resurrection. The death and resurrection of Lazarus, in a sense, brought on the death of Jesus. It prompted His enemies to move more quickly than they might have otherwise. By what He said and did at the death and resurrection of Lazarus, Jesus indicated what His death and resurrection would mean to His followers. Everything in this amazing event points ahead to Calvary and the open tomb.

5 The Plot against Him Thickens (11:45–57)

Many of the friends from Jerusalem believed in Jesus after He raised Lazarus. Some even told the Pharisees what had happened, perhaps hoping to convince them that Jesus was the Christ. Instead, learning of this miracle only accelerated their determination to get rid of Him. They met with the chief priests.

"He is a serious problem—a threat to our nation," they argued. "His group of followers continues to grow as a result of these miracles. If this continues, the Romans will crush them as a revolutionary movement. And the rest of us will be crushed along with them. Our city and our temple will be lost."

One of them, Caiaphas, the high priest, had it all figured out. "How ignorant can you be?" he chided. "This doesn't have to happen. All we have to do is have Him killed, and we're safe. The nation, the city, the temple, and we, ourselves—all saved if He dies! Doesn't that make sense? Isn't it better for one man to die than for the whole nation to perish?"

There was far more truth to what Caiaphas said than he ever imagined. Even on this occasion God spoke through him. In the circle of Jesus' worst enemies, while they were plotting His death, Caiaphas prophesied that He would die to rescue and unite not only the Jews, but all people.

Aware of the plot, Jesus and His disciples withdrew to the desert again for a short time. As Passover drew near, crowds from the country gathered in Jerusalem. There was much discussion and curiosity about Jesus. They knew about some of the amazing things He had said and done. They also had heard that His enemies wanted to arrest Him. "Will He come to the Feast?" they wondered. "Or will fear of His enemies keep Him away?"

Concluding Activities

Ask participants to read John 11:25 aloud together in a triumphant tone. (If participants have different translations, this will not affect the effectiveness of the exercise.) Then speak a brief prayer thanking God for His blessings given through this LifeLight course.

Make any necessary announcements. (You may want to announce the next LifeLight course. If it is to begin soon, you may want to distribute study leaflets for the course to all those whom have committed themselves to participate.)

Small-Group Leaders Material

The Messenger Is the Message

John 1:1–18

Preparing for the Session

Central Focus

God became a human being in order to make Himself known to us and to establish a personal relationship with us.

Objectives

That participants, by the power of the Holy Spirit working through the Word,

1. become increasingly aware that the Jesus whom they will meet in the Gospel is God in person, communicating His love to them;

2. receive Him in joyful and grateful faith as they experience Him in Word and deed;

3. grow in their personal relationship with Him as they participate in His life and ministry.

For the Small-Group Leader

As you read the discussion helps in preparation for the session, underline comments you will want to review before the discussion session and jot down other notes. You might want to preview all the lessons so that, if you should run across something that would aid you as a discussion leader (a newspaper article on AIDS for session 4 or a special tract on grieving for session 9), you can file it away and use it at the appropriate time.

As the discussion leader you are not expected to be the expert theologian and teacher. You are expected only to be the discussion leader, the one who keeps the discussion moving, encouraging and assisting all group members to take part in the discussion. A good discussion leader always directs the participants' attention to the Word of God, the one and only reliable authority. Remember the words found in the Gospel itself, "The Spirit gives life; the flesh counts for nothing. The words

I have spoken to you are spirit and they are life" (John 6:63).

The discussion helps should aid you in understanding the study questions and the answers the author is seeking. Study questions are numbered sequentially for the week so that any one question can be located quickly and easily. Explain to the participants that in each leaflet a challenge question is given, which is a more difficult, time-consuming question than usual—and is therefore optional.

In many cases, participants will not have had an opportunity to prepare for the first session; they will receive the study leaflet as they arrive. Take a few minutes at the beginning to give time for each participant to introduce himself or herself. Then you will work through the discussion questions as a group. There will probably be more than enough questions to fill the 55-minute small-group discussion period. Answer as many questions as time permits. You may want to save a few minutes to review the LifeLight process at the end, if at least some of the participants in your discussion group are new to LifeLight.

Though you are not expected to be the expert, you and the entire class will benefit if you show enthusiasm for the study. Let your excitement for the study of God's Word serve as a catalyst to excite the other participants. Call the participants' attention to the opening thought in their student leaflets.

Small-Group Discussion Helps

Distribute name tags as participants arrive. Help group members get acquainted. This will be an important part of the first session unless all of the members of the group are already known to one another. Be sensitive to any new members who might be attending for the first time, especially if all of the other members of the class have been together in previous LifeLight studies.

One way to open the participants up as they introduce themselves is to have each person share a "peak experience" in the past month. Be sure to define what is meant by a peak experience. It is simply a high point in one's life. (For example, "My peak experience was when I got married this past month!") If it is too difficult for some to come up with such an experience over the past month, ask them to think of any peak experience in the past year or so.

In addition to learning names, you may want to ask group members to tell the others something about themselves—their families, occupations, special interests, or other information they may wish to share. Getting acquainted is an important goal for this session—be sure to spend some time for this.

The Purpose of John's Gospel

A quick glance at John's Gospel shows that it is unique in that it contains no parables. Like the other three Gospels, John's Gospel records many of Jesus' miracles and His personal conversations. However, it does not record the Christmas story; that is found only in Luke's Gospel (the coming of the Wise Men is in Matthew). Neither does John record the institution of the Lord's Supper or Jesus' baptism. It should be noted that John's Gospel does record some events the other Gospels do not: changing the water into wine at Cana; Jesus' conversations with Nicodemus and the woman of Samaria; the raising of Lazarus; and Jesus' discourses with His disciples during the final week in Jerusalem.

1. Many participants may refer to or recite John 3:16: "For God so loved the world that He gave His one and only Son, that whoever believes in Him shall not perish but have eternal life."

2. It is evident from John 20:30–31 that the purpose of the author is to lead people to saving faith in Christ as the Son of God and so to have eternal life.

3. John shows the deity of Christ throughout the Gospel by describing some of the miraculous signs of Jesus. John 2:1–11 describes Jesus' first miracle, changing water into wine. John 11:38–44 records the miracle of bringing Lazarus back to life. John records the miracles to attest Jesus' messiahship so that people "may believe that Jesus is the Christ, the Son of God, and that by believing [they] may have life in His name" (John 20:31).

4. John draws some exciting word pictures of Jesus. (a) John 8:58—I AM. Hundreds of years before Jesus said

this, God was called by the same name. Moses had been called to lead His people out of Egypt. Frightened, "Moses said to God, 'Suppose I go to the Israelites and say to them, "The God of your fathers has sent me to you," and they ask me, "What is His name?" Then what shall I tell them?' God said to Moses, 'I AM WHO I AM. This is what you are to say to the Israelites: "I AM has sent me to you"'" (Exodus 3:13–14). In Hebrew I AM comes from the same root word as Yahweh. Yahweh may mean "He is" or "He will make things happen." The name Yahweh became so sacred and awesome that the Hebrews would not even speak the word aloud.

Jesus said "I AM . . ." 22 times in the Gospel of John. Jesus used the words to inform His audience time and time again that He was God Himself come in the flesh, and He spoke with the authority of *Yahweh*, the Lord. Knowing that He is "I AM" makes His other statements come alive. Repeatedly, He used the phrase in making His personal promises to us. "I am the way and the truth and the life" (14:6). "I am the Good Shepherd" (10:11). "I am the resurrection and the life. He who believes in Me will live, even though he dies; and whoever lives and believes in Me will never die" (11:25–26). In John 8 some of the leaders of Israel challenged Jesus' statement that He had come to make them free (vv. 31–33). Jesus informed them that He was not only the God of Abraham and responsible for His calling and promises in the past but also the promised Messiah *now,* who had been sent to call them and make promises to them.

Other word pictures are (b) John 6:35—bread of life; (c) John 10:11—good shepherd; (d) John 11:25—resurrection and the life; (e) John 14:6—the way and the truth and the life; (f) John 15:1—true vine.

5. The word *synoptic* means "a seeing together." All the Gospels help us see a total picture of Jesus' ministry. All of them are unique and essential for making disciples of the Lord. Without the Gospel of John, it would be difficult for us to comprehend completely why there was so much opposition to Jesus and why His opponents eventually put Him to death. John's is the only Gospel that records some of Jesus' previous visits to Jerusalem before His final entry. Each time Jesus went to Jerusalem, John reports great opposition.

For centuries the symbol of this Gospel has been the eagle. It was the bird thought to soar the highest and come closest to knowing and seeing the brightness of the sun. The Gospel of John can provide for you a closer and brighter view of God. (a) The Gospel purpose was also very practical. Jesus came that we "may have life, and have it to the full" (John 10:10). (b) This record shows that faith in Jesus made a difference in the lives of the people, from the changing of water into wine at the wedding feast to the raising of Lazarus from the dead. Encourage participants to put into their own words the great difference that Jesus' coming makes.

About the Author

6. John's father was Zebedee (Mark 1:19–20).

7. John and his brother James responded immediately to Jesus' calling by leaving their nets and following Him.

8. (a) John and his brother were called Sons of Thunder (Mark 3:17). (b) The nickname was more than fitting, especially considering their anger toward a village of people who refused to receive Christ and His disciples. They were so angry that they wanted to call fire down from heaven and burn the people to death (Luke 9:51–54).

9. Though John was known as a Son of Thunder, he was greatly loved by Jesus. A poignant example of Jesus' love is seen when Jesus asks John to take Jesus' mother home and treat her as his own (John 19:26–27).

10. The three disciples who were in Jesus' inner circle were Peter, James, and John.

The Messenger Is the Message

Remind the participants that God became a human being in order to make Himself known to us and to establish a personal relationship with us. Direct their attention to the second Bible memorization verse, John 1:14: "The Word became flesh and made His dwelling among us. We have seen His glory, the glory of the One and Only, who came from the Father, full of grace and truth." The messenger, God, actually is the message, the Word in the flesh.

11. The prologue presents all the essential ideas of the Gospel. It clearly states who Christ is, what He did, and for what purpose He came. A study of the key words in the prologue will help the participants understand the valuable message of John's Gospel.

Word. (a) Jesus is the Word. He was in the beginning and created all things. He is with God and actually is God (vv. 1–2). (b) The Word (Jesus) was with God from the beginning; in fact, He is God. (c) The world did not recognize or acknowledge Jesus, the Word, as its God. (d) He "made His dwelling among us" so that we might see "His glory, the glory of the One and Only, who came from the Father, full of grace and truth" (v. 14). (e) Genesis 1:3, 6, 9 and Colossians 1:16 tell us that the Word created everything. Jonah 1:1–2 tells us that the Word directed the prophets. Psalm 107:19–20 tells us that the Word brought healing. Isaiah 55:10–11 promises that the Word always brings about some results. The Word never returns empty.

Light. (f) The "true light" who came into the world is Jesus. He "gives light to every man" (v. 9). (g) John 1:6–7 tells us that John the Baptist had been commissioned to witness to the coming of Jesus, the light. God's own people, however, the people of Israel, did not respond positively to John's message or to Jesus' coming. Sadly, "Light has come into the world, but men loved darkness instead of light because their deeds were evil" (John 3:19).

Life. (h) Life and light are closely related because light gives life. It is essential for existence, both physical and spiritual. Jesus, our light, is essential for our eternal existence. Christ's gift is life, life eternal, and life more abundant (John 10:10).

Believe. (i) To believe means to accept as true or real, to trust with the full confidence of the heart. (j) We become children of God by believing in His name, by believing that He is true and real, trusting in Him as the one appointed by God as the Savior.

Grace. (k) Jesus, who had become flesh, revealed grace and truth. Both words are primary characteristics of God. (l) Grace is God's unmerited favor (love) for His people.

Truth. (m) Verse 17 contrasts the Law and what Jesus Christ did. The Law and all its regulations may be true, but it is not a truth that frees. The truth that Jesus reveals is that God forgives us and accepts us for the sake of Jesus, our Redeemer. Jesus Christ is Himself the truth. "I am the way and the truth and the life. No one comes to the Father except through Me" (John 14:6).

12. We know God only through Jesus Christ.

A Few Reminders for Your Upcoming LifeLight Studies

Review for the participants that each future LifeLight study leaflet will contain an opening thought, Bible verses for memorization, resources for worship, prayer suggestions for the week, enrichment activities, and Bible study.

After reading the explanations given in the study leaflet for each part, ask if there are any questions. Remind the participants that the opening thought, Bible verses for memorization, prayer suggestions for the week, and enrichment activities are suggestions of things to think about and activities to do during the week. Though they are optional, if done, they promise to help the participants in their walk with the Lord.

Review how the weekly assemblies are scheduled: opening worship (5 minutes); small-group discussions (55 minutes); lecture (20 minutes); closing activities (5 minutes). Participants will receive an enrichment magazine at their first session and a new study leaflet at the close of each session, for use in the next week's session.

Remind the participants that the journey will not always be easy. The course calls for disciplined, regular study so that God can work His message into their hearts. At times they may not feel like studying, or they may not have ample time each week to finish the lessons. Encourage participants to finish each day's lesson; however, remind them that even if they do not complete all the lessons, they are to be sure to come to class each week.

At other times the devil may tempt them to get sidetracked during the lecture or bring about a personality clash with another participant. Our sinful nature often conspires with Satan to derail the good that is promised through the study of God's Word. Remind the participants that God's Spirit is stronger. God has promised that His Word will not return to Him void but will accomplish His purpose.

Conclude by quoting John 20:31: May we together, through this study, "believe that Jesus is the Christ, the Son of God, and that by believing [we] may have life in His name."

Introducing the Messenger

John 1:19–2:25

Preparing for the Session

Central Focus

At first Jesus is introduced by others, and then He introduces Himself.

Objectives

That participants, by the power of the Holy Spirit working through the Word,

1. realize that then and now Jesus chooses to be introduced by others;

2. accept the high privilege of directing others to Him;

3. are attentive and responsive when others direct them to Jesus;

4. eagerly anticipate personal encounters with God as they study and share Jesus through the Gospel of John;

5. because of their faith relationship with Jesus, recognize God's love at work in His creation in both ordinary and miraculous ways;

6. respond with humility and contrition when the loving God expresses judgment on them for their sins.

For the Small-Group Leader

Everyone in your group should have become acquainted at last week's study. If someone new has joined this week, take a few minutes to introduce the person to the rest of the group. Even if there are no new people, it might be wise to have everyone introduce themselves again. Be especially watchful of groups of people who may be cliquish because they've had previous associations in the church. It is easy for new people to feel unwanted. Encourage a warm, friendly, accepting attitude in your group.

You can expect some to speak more than others. Make sure that no one consistently dominates the group discussion. Provide opportunities for less talkative participants to contribute when they show interest. Never let them feel foolish for asking what they might call a "dumb question." Encourage questions of all kinds, simple or complex.

As the discussion leader, you will quickly detect who may be apprehensive about reading in class. Never ask someone to read who might feel uncomfortable doing so. To determine who these people might be, begin by asking for volunteers. **(It's not a bad idea to have all reading done by volunteers.)**

Announce to the class that in every Bible study there are people at different levels of Bible knowledge. Some may know where the different books of the Bible are; others may not even know that Genesis is the first book of the Bible. Assure the group that it doesn't make any difference because we are all here together to learn. What is most important is that we want to grow in faith.

The agenda for the discussion groups is to review the study questions the participants answered at home during the week. While more time will and should be given to areas of greater concern or interest, try not to get bogged down. There may be times when there are unresolved questions. Don't be afraid to say that you simply don't know the answer and will do some research for next week. Write down the unresolved questions, and don't hesitate to ask the pastor or other spiritual leaders in the church for help.

Remember, encourage the members to come even if they don't complete all of the lesson; however, remind them that each one will get as much out of it as is put into it. Some of that depends on daily preparation. As an effective group leader, you must be an example by faithfully preparing each week. This means that you will have done each day's work yourself.

As you begin lesson 2, you may want to review the opening thought and make sure that everyone understands how it ties in with this week's lesson. Just as the large dog had brought back to the doctor's home another dog who had been injured, so the same thing happened when Jesus began His ministry. One person after another brought others with them to meet Jesus (for example, Andrew introduced his brother to Jesus).

Small Group Discussion Helps

Day 1 • John 1:19–28

1. "Who are you?" (vv. 19, 22). Everyone was talking about the new preacher in the area, who was baptizing all kinds of people as a sign of repentance; therefore, the Jews sent a delegation of priests and Levites to ask John some questions. Since they had long awaited the promised Messiah, they had to check out John's credentials. Some obviously wondered if perhaps John was the Messiah.

2. (a) John answered the delegation of questioners, stating unequivocally that he was not the Messiah (v. 20). The questioners pursued other possibilities. "Are you Elijah?" (v. 21). They may have been thinking of God's Word in Mark 4:5–6, where it was promised Elijah would return "before that great and dreadful day of the Lord comes." (b) Though he stated decisively that he was not a reincarnation of Elijah, John came to minister in the "spirit and power of Elijah" (Luke 1:17). (c) John identified himself by words from Isaiah 40:3: "I am the voice of one calling in the desert, 'Make straight the way for the Lord' " (v. 23). He was a "voice," calling on people to prepare the way for the promised Messiah by repenting of their sins, by showing their repentance in receiving John's baptism, and by looking in faith for God to fulfill His promises by sending the long-expected Messiah.

3. If he was only a voice, the Pharisees reasoned, then why did he baptize? They only saw baptism as a way of cleansing proselytes, Gentile converts, and yet John was obviously baptizing both Jews and proselytes. John appeared to make no distinction between the Gentiles and sinners and God's chosen people, the Jews. The proud Pharisees objected to such a procedure.

4. (a) John stated he would not loosen the Messiah's sandal thong (v. 27), because he was not worthy to do it. In other words, he did not consider himself worthy to

be the Messiah's slave. John the Baptist recognized it was his mission to elevate Jesus: John's humility is clearly seen in John 1:27. John confessed his own unworthiness, as a sinner, before his Lord. (b) Help participants explore opportunities available to them in their own lives to show humility in their service to God and to other people.

Day 2 • John 1:29–34

5. (a) John the Baptist introduced Jesus by using imagery the people were very familiar with, especially since they were about to celebrate the Passover. During the special celebration of Passover they would offer as a sacrifice a Passover lamb (Exodus 12:21). Perhaps at this very moment flocks of sheep could be seen coming across the rolling hills to Jerusalem for the special national holiday. Amidst all this activity, John the Baptist pointed to Jesus and declared Him to be "the Lamb of God, who takes away the sin of the world" (v. 29). (b) **Challenge question.** Genesis 22:8—As Abraham took his son Isaac to a sacrifice at which, though he did not know it, Isaac was himself to be the victim, Isaac asked about the missing sacrificial lamb. Abraham quietly replied that God Himself would provide it. And so He did. In place of Isaac God provided a ram for the sacrifice that day. That ram represented Christ, whom God would put forward as a sacrifice not only for Isaac but for all. Exodus 12:1–3 and 1 Corinthians 5:7—The Passover lamb's blood, smeared over the doors of Israelite homes, shielded God's people from the destroying angel; its flesh, eaten by the Israelites in those homes, promised coming deliverance. Christ is our Passover Lamb; His blood shields us from God's just wrath, and His flesh delivers us from the slavery of sin. Isaiah 53:4–7—Isaiah foretold that God's Servant would bear the punishment due to God's wandering sheep, silently suffering for our sins. He is the sacrificial Lamb God appointed.

6. Jesus was to become the sacrificial lamb, who would be offered for the sin of the world. The perfect sacrifice of Jesus did not have to be repeated year after year as did the sacrifices of lambs or bulls or goats. His sacrifice cleansed us "from acts that lead to death, so that we may serve the living God" (Hebrews 9:14). He redeemed us with His precious blood (1 Peter 1:19).

7. John the Baptist directed people to Jesus, "the Lamb of God who takes away the sin of the world" (John 1:29). We are to be like John the Baptist; all our witness must focus on Jesus. This witness must be more than living a Christian life. It must include a verbal witness, especially since we recognize that the Word along with the Sacraments are ways in which God's grace is given to people. In order to witness verbally, we must know very clearly from scripture about whom we are witnessing. We need to clarify in a concise, scriptural way who Jesus Christ is, what He has done, and how His grace and mercy become ours.

8. There are many points of contact between the baptism of John and the Baptism we have experienced. Both baptisms center in Jesus. The recipients of John's baptism and we obtained forgiveness of our sins through baptism; this forgiveness was won for us, as it would be won for people in John's day, on the cross of Jesus. As John himself pointed out, and as the apostles affirmed, we also receive the gift of the Holy Spirit in Baptism. This Spirit received in Baptism enables us to believe in our hearts that Jesus is our Savior and to profess our faith in Him. We should not pit John's baptism against the Baptism we have received; both were established by God to pour the gift of grace won by Christ into our hearts and daily lives by faith.

Day 3 • John 1:35–51

9. (a) John the Baptist points to Jesus as "the Lamb of God" (vv. 35–36). (b) Andrew says Jesus is the "Messiah" (v. 41). (c) Philip speaks of Jesus as the fulfillment of what the prophets wrote (v. 45). (d) Nathanael proclaimed Him to be the "Son of God" and the "King of Israel" (v. 49).

10. You can almost feel Andrew's excitement when he tells his brother he has found the Messiah. If a brother or sister or some family member of ours is not a Christian, God gives us the privilege and responsibility to witness to them. Church growth studies have shown that 70–90 percent of all converts are brought to Christ by someone they trust, such as a personal friend or a family member. Do not ask participants to share their answers to this question. If, however, someone asks for counsel or prayers, be sure to rally the support of the class.

11. Jesus knew all about Nathanael even though they had never met. This assured Nathanael that Jesus was the Messiah. Jesus has to be God, for, after all, only God knows all things (Psalm 139). In Hebrews we read that Jesus "is the radiance of God's glory and the exact representation of His being" (Hebrews 1:3). (a) Knowing Jesus knows all things is comforting because it assures us He knows our strengths and our weaknesses, our abilities and our inadequacies. Because of this knowledge we know He can and will take care of our every need. Knowing Jesus knows all things can be disturbing if we think we can hide anything from Him. In your group, remind one another that even though Jesus knows everything about us, including our sins, He still loves us. Though Jesus knew everything about the adulterous woman, He loved her and forgave her. Jesus came to reconcile us to our heavenly Father. Though the prodigal son had abandoned his father, the father had not abandoned his son. "But while he was still a long way off, his father saw him and was filled with compassion for him; he ran to his son, threw his arms around him and kissed him" (Luke 15:20). John 3:16 reminds us that God, our Father, "so loved the [sinful] world that He gave His one and only Son." (b) By His cross, Jesus bridges the gap between sinful humans and a holy God. God spoke to Jacob's loneliness and fear with the vision of a stairway and ministering angels. He thereby told a guilty Jacob that He forgave him. God our Father can and does forgive us because Jesus through His death has become our mediator—our reconciling stairway—to God. God's ministering angels now minister to us who are God's children, even as in Jacob's vision they were seen going from God to Jacob.

Day 4 • John 2:1–11

12. Jesus came to earth not only to give us eternal life but to give us life more abundant. Jesus tells us, "I have come that they may have life, and have it to the full" (John 10:10). Jesus always makes a difference in people's lives, including the lives of those who are married and are walking with the Lord.

Christ graciously and bountifully takes care of those who invite Him and desire His blessings. Marriages, families, and relationships are all made happier when Jesus is included. Ask participants to list some practical ways in which the Gospel enhances and improves family life. Some might mention the love we experience from God and learn to share with others, the forgiveness we offer one another for Jesus' sake, the peace Christ places in our hearts that flows out from us into our relationships, and the way Christians learn to place the interests of others before their own.

13. At first glance Jesus' answer did not seem to be very kind: "Dear woman, why do you involve Me? . . . My time has not yet come" (v. 4). It was unusual for a son to address his mother as "woman." But Jesus intended no disrespect toward Mary. He was perhaps indicating a more independent relationship as He began His public ministry. "Let me do this in My way. The time for showing My power to the world has not yet arrived."

14. "Do whatever He tells you" became the catalyst for the miracle at Cana. Such is the catalyst for miracles in our lives as well. It is important we not only trust God, but that we also obey Him. Jesus Himself said, "If you hold to My teaching, you are really My disciples" (John 8:31).

15. By changing the water to wine Jesus revealed His glory, and His disciples put their faith in Him. The revelation of Himself as the Son of God, who had come into the world to save us and to cause people to put their faith in Him as their Savior, was the purpose of all of Jesus' miracles that would follow.

Day 5 • John 2:12–25

16. The temple was a place for people to meet God and to hear His Word, especially the promises of the coming Savior—not a place for commercial transactions, and particularly not transactions where people were cheated (Mark 11:17).

17. (a) He answered their questions with a proclamation using the imagery at hand, that of the temple. Jesus said, "Destroy this temple, and I wild raise it again in three days" (v. 19). (b) He prophesied (though His audience certainly did not understand) that though He would be killed, in three days He would be raised back to life (vv. 21–22). (c) The response of His audience is no surprise. Thinking He was speaking about their temple of worship, they taunted Him by saying that the temple had taken 46 years to build, and to think He

could rebuild it in three days was ridiculous. Later, Jesus' words (or the misrepresentation of them) were thrown back at Him at His trial and at His crucifixion. Even after Jesus had returned to heaven, His opponents continued to mock Him with these words.

18. Many things can corrupt present day worship. Thoughtless ritual, meaningless ceremony, or rote prayers could do it. So could displacing worship as the church's central activity with fellowship or social activities. Even commercial considerations could become central in church decisions and activities. Perhaps participants will think of other ways in which the church might be distracted from its real purpose or even corrupted.

19. Many of the disciples were impressed with Jesus' miracles but still didn't accept Him as the Messiah. They had not committed themselves to Him. Jesus knew what was really in their hearts. Jesus, therefore, "did not entrust Himself to them" (v. 24).

20. As time permits allow participants to share affirmations or insights from the week's study. Close the session with a brief prayer.

One-on-One

John 3:1–4:42

Preparing for the Session

Central Focus

Jesus communicates powerfully with two very different individuals, inviting and drawing them into a personal and saving relationship with God.

Objectives

That participants, by the power of the Holy Spirit working through the Word,

1. recognize that the God of the universe communicates and relates intimately with them as individuals;

2. are prepared to receive from Him even more than they expect;

3. make the focus of their faith Jesus, as He in love gives Himself for the life of the world;

4. reach out to others and invite them into a one-on-one relationship with Him.

For the Small-Group Leader

As you continue your role as discussion leader, joyfully trust God's Spirit. He has ways of working even through your inadequacies. The theme for lesson 3 is "One-on-One." Jesus communicates powerfully with two very different individuals. In the same way, Jesus communicates to each one of us that He loves us, no matter how different we might be. Call special attention to the powerful lesson on evangelism as Jesus communicates to the Samaritan woman. When discussing the different levels of communication, help participants analyze their levels of communication with God. Remind them that all sorts of good things happen when there is honest communication, not only with people, but with God as well. Encourage them to use the different prayer suggestions given each week on the first page of each study leaflet. As group members become better acquainted with one another, they are more comfortable opening up to each other, sharing special needs and concerns. As these needs or expressions of joy are made known, don't hesitate, if it seems appropriate, to offer a special prayer, focusing on the joy or concern expressed.

When instances of sadness or failure are related, keep a positive, Gospel-centered spirit uppermost in the discussion. Always make sure that the Gospel of Christ, with its words of forgiveness and victory, has the last word.

Small-Group Discussion Helps

Day 1 • John 3:1–15

1. Jesus was referring to Baptism. At this time Baptism was part of the ministry of Jesus through His disciples, as we see in John 3:22 and 4:1–2. Paul (in Romans 6:4) speaks of Baptism as a new life (a being born again) that occurs following death; this death and new life come through faith in Jesus. Paul also (in 1 Corinthians 6:11) speaks of Baptism as being washed, justified, and sanctified through faith in Christ. To be "born again" means to start over, to have a new beginning. This new beginning comes about when we leave our sin behind us, by faith nailed to Jesus' cross and done away with, and begin living a new life that loves God and follows the direction of the Holy Spirit. Encourage participants to put this reality in their own lives into their own words.

2. Scripture is clear that we are by nature spiritually dead and not at all receptive to God's grace. The Good News is that we are saved by God's grace. Faith is God's doing. (a) In Romans 9:16 we learn that our salvation is a result of God's mercy, not of human effort. (b) 2 Corinthians 4:6 tells us how God made the light of the Gospel shine into our hearts just as surely as He caused light to shine at the beginning of creation. (c) Ephesians 2:1, 5, 8–10 teaches us that by nature we were dead in sin but that God in His grace has made us

alive. We receive salvation entirely as a gift, not as a result of our work. But being saved means that we yield to God's plan to make of us glad doers of good works.

3. **Challenge question.** (a) The prophet Daniel saw "one like a son of man" in a vision (Daniel 7:13). He saw that God, the Ancient of Days, gave this man authority, glory, and sovereign power, and all nations worshiped Him. God gave Him an everlasting kingdom. The prophecy Daniel was given in this vision is fulfilled in Jesus, who most often referred to Himself as the Son of Man. (b) Jesus, by being lifted up on the cross, saved all mankind from the sting of sin, eternal death. Just as all of the snake-bitten Israelites were delivered from the serpents' deadly venom by looking in faith to the bronze serpent on the pole, so all who are suffering from the poisonous venom of sin are healed and saved when they look in faith to Christ on His cross. A perfect summary is given in verses 14–15: "Just as Moses lifted up the snake in the desert, so the Son of Man must be lifted up, that everyone who believes in Him may have eternal life."

Day 2 • John 3:16–21

4. In 1 Corinthians 13:4–8 St. Paul describes the kind of love God's people have for one another. This love is God-given. It is a deliberate, selfless love.

5. God sent His Son, Jesus, into the world to save us (a) from God's wrath because of sin and (b) from the power of the devil to devour us.

6. Emphasize that God our Father loves all people (the world, John 3:16). Christ died for the whole world. He did not want anyone to perish but have everlasting life. Still, "Everyone who does evil hates the light, and will not come into the light for fear that his deeds will be exposed. But whoever lives by the truth comes into the light, so that it may be seen plainly that what he has done has been done through God" (vv. 20–21). Sometimes people stay away from church because they fear that God's Word of Law will accuse and expose them of their wrongdoing. In fact, the Law does expose the wrongdoing of all of us. The point: We need to be aware of our sin so that we may all the more firmly cling to God's forgiveness in Christ. God's Law, the Ten Commandments, is like a searchlight exposing our sin. But the Lord will cleanse and heal those who come in

repentance and faith into the light of the Gospel.

7. Jesus Himself is the truth by which we live as we put our faith in Him for forgiveness, life, and strength. We find our Lord Jesus in God's Word, the Gospel, revealed to us in the Holy Scriptures.

8. There is no logical explanation why God loved us so much that He gave up His only Son into death so that our sins might not destroy us. 1 John 4:8–9 tells us that God is love. It's one of His defining attributes. St. Paul prayed, "And I pray that you, being rooted and established in love, may have power, together with all the saints, to grasp how wide and long and high and deep is the love of Christ, and to know this love that surpasses knowledge that you may be filled to the measure of all the fullness of God" (Ephesians 3:17–19). In speaking to someone about God's love, the best we can do is simply keep on pointing to Christ. Christ is God's love in action—for our salvation.

Day 3 • John 3:22–36

9. God and His people are often pictured in a marriage relationship. (a) The people of God, whether in the Old Testament or the New Testament, are the bride. (b) Jesus is the bridegroom, or husband. (c) John the Baptist considered himself the friend of the bridegroom. The friend of the bridegroom prepared and led the bride to her bridegroom.

10. John the Baptist, as he prepares God's people to receive God's gift of the Messiah, reveals three important truths about the Savior, truths that Jesus also taught in His ministry as it followed that of John. (a) Jesus the Messiah came down to earth from heaven. He is not of the earth, as are all other people, but He is of heaven. (b) As Jesus the Messiah is of heaven, not of the earth, He speaks a message that comes directly from God; it does not result from human thought or reasoning but is God's own revelation of heavenly truth to the people of this earth. (c) Jesus the Messiah will save from sin and death all who receive this heavenly message for what it is, believe it, and live by it. This heavenly message saves them, and no one can take this message and salvation from them. Those who reject this heavenly message, however, will be lost and will experience eternal death. What a powerful affirmation with which John introduced Jesus to the world!

11. Our response must always be based on the Scriptures. All of John 3 would help demonstrate clearly the hope of a Christian, but especially verses 15–16 and 36.

Day 4 • John 4:1–26

12. (a) The people of Israel, the Northern Kingdom, were conquered and carried off into exile by the Assyrians in 722 B.C. The Assyrian king, Shalmaneser V, repopulated the country with people from other lands he had conquered (and who had been exiled from their own native lands). By this policy the Assyrian rulers sought to pacify conquered nations and prevent them from rising up against their conquerors. Unlike the Judeans, who were to be conquered and exiled by the Babylonians approximately 135 years later, the people of the Northern Kingdom were never to return to their homeland. The new inhabitants merged the worship of God with their own pagan religions, particularly as they intermarried with Israelites who had been left behind. The Jews refused to accept the Samaritans (as they came to be called, after their capital, Samaria) as worshipers of God but regarded them as Gentile unbelievers. (b) Orthodox Jews would avoid going through Samaria because it was filled with a mixed race of people. Nevertheless, Jesus "had to go through Samaria" because of a divine compulsion. He knew there was someone who had a great spiritual need in Samaria, and so He had no choice but to stop in this forbidden city. As the Good Shepherd, He seeks out His sheep wherever they may be.

13. (a) He started out with small talk by asking for a drink of water, verse 7. (b) He refused to argue, even though the woman attempted to do so several times. She first asked why He would ask her for a drink of water since she was a Samaritan woman (v. 9). She wanted to argue about the whole racial issue between the Jews and the Samaritans. Jesus made it clear He wasn't going to argue about this issue, nor about the second issue she raised, that of where to worship (vv. 19–20). As we witness to other people, it is easy for us to be drawn into arguments about unimportant issues and to lose focus on what is most important, one's relationship to Jesus Christ. (c) Jesus steered the woman back to what was important by arousing her interest. He suggested He had something she didn't even know about, a

"living" water that would keep her from thirsting ever again (vv. 10, 13). (d) The woman had a great need. Jesus helped awaken that need by asking that she call her husband (v. 16). The question opened up the woman's past. She was living with someone, but he wasn't her husband. The question also made her recall her five unsuccessful attempts at marriage. Jesus very subtly and quietly opened up her past so that she would recognize how much she needed what He had to offer, forgiveness and salvation. (e) Jesus announced He was the promised Messiah (v. 26). He was the "living water" who had come to bring "eternal life" (vv. 10, 13). Witness must always end with Jesus as being the only solution for the problems of sin and death.

14. Like the Samaritan woman, we often try to avoid talking about our sinfulness. Jesus always confronts us for one reason, to lead us to repentance.

Day 5 • John 4:27–42

15. Most of the supporting verses would indicate that the Samaritan woman did respond positively to Jesus' ministry. (a) The fact that the woman left the water jar indicated she was excited, too excited to think about anything but the "living water." (b) Jesus had made a definite impression on the woman in that He told her everything she had done. She asked others whether they thought He might be the Christ, perhaps wanting them to say yes to reaffirm what she already believed. (c) The woman must have been convincing, because many "believed in Him" because of her testimony.

16. Jesus is so taken up with His mission that He needs and wants to do the Father's will, even as we need and want and hunger for food. The metaphor simply communicates how totally and single-heartedly Jesus dedicates Himself to doing and finishing His work of our redemption (John 19:30).

17. His trip to Samaria proved that the harvest was great. Everywhere there were people who had great spiritual needs. Everywhere there were people who needed "living water." "Open your eyes and look at the fields! They are ripe for harvest," Jesus told the people. The harvest is just as great today.

18. The fields are ripe where we live as well. Everywhere there are people who thirst for something more. They

are spiritually dry and empty. (a) Don't ask anyone to share, but be ready to offer your support and prayers, and the support and prayers of the group, as the participants think of people in their circle of friends who are spiritually thirsty. (b) You might want to offer a prayer now asking that God would help them make a bold witness to the people they have identified.

Communication through Healing

John 4:43–5:47

Preparing for the Session

Central Focus

Jesus communicates divine love by compassionately responding to the need for healing.

Objectives

That participants, by the power of the Holy Spirit working through the Word,

1. discover in Jesus' healing activity (both miraculous and natural) that the God of the universe cares about their suffering and losses and is willing to do something about them;

2. confidently ask for help when they face such needs;

3. notice and gratefully celebrate His answers to prayer for such help;

4. trust that if God does not give them what they ask for, He will give them something even better;

5. acknowledge penitently their negligence in asking for His help and/or in giving thanks for His marvelous response to their needs;

6. interpret every act of His physical care as an expression of His saving love.

For the Small-Group Leader

Lesson 4 focuses on how Jesus communicates His divine love by responding compassionately to the need for healing. Remind the group that though Jesus may not always give physical healing even when we fervently pray for it, He has given each of us the most important healing—spiritual healing. Through His own life, death, and resurrection Jesus has given us forgiveness and eternal life. Avoid thinking you must have an answer for every question asked. The discussion leader does what a fishing guide does—guides!

Small-Group Discussion Helps

Day 1 • John 4:43–54

1. They welcomed Jesus because of the things "He had done in Jerusalem." Unfortunately, time showed that many of them welcomed Him for exploitive reasons. They wanted some special favor or miracle.

2. Our relationship with Jesus may also become exploitive when we want the gift but not the giver. We want what Jesus has to offer, but we don't want Jesus to rule and govern our lives. We want to get what we can from Him but give nothing in return.

3. "Your son will live," Jesus assured the official (v. 50). It was for this reason Jesus had come. "I have come that they may have life" (John 10:10).

4. He wanted to confirm that the healing was linked with Jesus' words—and was indeed accomplished by Jesus. Whenever God spoke, things happened, as in creation when He said, "Let there be," and there was.

5. Jesus speaks to our own weak faith, which may be afraid to take Him at His word, and through this miracle of healing assures us that we can trust Him. If participants do not mention the following, suggest that we all can ask the Holy Spirit for a stronger faith, one more like that of the royal official when he "took Jesus at His word and departed" (v. 50). We can remember that we are baptized; be faithful in coming to the Lord's Table, expecting forgiveness and strengthening; and make the Holy Scriptures a part of each day. After all, Jesus gives us promise after promise in Scripture, and we can rely on these promises.

Day 2 • John 5:1–9

6. There are many significant differences between the healing of the paralyzed man at the pool of Bethesda (John 5:1–15) and the healing of the royal official's son (John 4:43–54). The royal official asked Jesus to heal his son, but no one asked Jesus to heal the paralyzed man; Jesus simply took notice of him and healed him.

The royal official showed faith in Jesus, though it was a faith that grew as the event moved along. No indication is given that the paralyzed man believed that Jesus would or could heal him; he did not even know who Jesus was (v. 13). Jesus healed the royal official's son at a distance; the paralyzed man was in Jesus' presence. The healing of the royal official's son did not involve Jesus in controversy as the healing of the paralyzed man did. Perhaps participants will find other differences they consider significant.

7. (a) Jesus' healing of the royal official's son encourages prayer on behalf of others. This event also shows Jesus' power; a simple word performed the miracle. This miracle may also be encouraging since the official evidenced an imperfect and growing faith, perhaps a faith we understand and to which we relate. (b) The healing of the paralyzed man might be encouraging in that it resolved a problem that had existed for a long while. Also, Jesus Himself recognized the need and helped, even though He had not been asked. Sometimes we do not even recognize what our real needs are. This miracle clearly did not depend on the paralyzed man's faith; he did not even recognize Jesus. How encouraging to us when we wonder whether our faith is strong enough to receive the Lord's help!

8. There were great numbers of "disabled people," meaning those unable to help themselves. Apart from Christ, everyone is "disabled." Insofar as we are sinners, we are "disabled people" also. (a) Our blindness is a spiritual blindness. Like Nicodemus, we cannot "see the kingdom of God unless [we are] born again" (John 3:3). (b) We are also spiritually lame. We cannot come to Christ, as some would suggest, "unless the Father . . . draws [us]" (John 6:44). (c) We are also spiritually paralyzed. Like St. Paul, we know what we are supposed to do, but we don't do it (Romans 7:18). Only through the Holy Spirit and His divine working in us can we do any good.

9. Encourage some of the class members to share their prayers.

Day 3 • John 5:10–15

10. (a) **Challenge question.** Exodus 20:8–10, the commandment about the Sabbath, forbade anyone in the Jewish household to do any work since God Himself rested on the seventh day after creating the universe. Nehemiah 13:15 tells how Nehemiah admonished those who carried on commercial activities on the Sabbath. In Jeremiah 17:27 God threatens to punish even those who come into Jerusalem to offer sacrifices if they carry loads through the city gates on the Sabbath. (b) When Jesus' opponents criticized His disciples for harvesting on the Sabbath (when they plucked heads of grain in a field to satisfy their hunger), Jesus pointed out how David had violated prohibitions of the law and fed his soldiers consecrated bread, lawful only for priests to eat. God never intended that the Sabbath should prohibit preservation of life or works of mercy. (c) The prohibition in Jeremiah of carrying a load did not apply to the healed man who was carrying his mat. Rather, the prohibitions regarding labor on the Sabbath were directed at commercial activities, by which people served themselves instead of acknowledging the Lord. God intended the Sabbath to assist people, not to burden them.

11. More than likely, Jesus slipped away because His time had not yet come (John 7:6). He had preparatory work to do before His crucifixion and resurrection. Had He stayed, the opposition and hatred would probably have intensified.

12. Sin and its consequence, eternal death. Jesus may have given this warning to the man because he did not have a saving faith, as suggested, perhaps, by verse 13.

13. Now the man knew who had healed him physically and spiritually—Jesus! The focus of our witness must always be on Jesus and on what He has done for us, whether we are speaking of a physical or a spiritual healing.

Day 4 • John 5:16–30

14. Jesus dared to say He was doing God's work! Realizing that Jesus was calling Himself God, the Jews saw Him as the ultimate blasphemer.

15. **Challenge question.** Jesus reaches out in compassion and mercy through Word and Sacrament.

16. Though Jesus does not directly, at this time, say He is equal to the Father, He says it indirectly. (a) Verse 19—He does what the Father does; (b) verse 20—the Father revealed to the Son everything; (c) verse 21—like

the Father He gives life; (d) verse 22—judgment has also been entrusted to Jesus; (e) verse 23—honor is due Him, just as to the Father; (f) verse 24—like the Father, He gives eternal life.

Day 5 • John 5:31–47

17. Many witnesses came forward to testify on Jesus' behalf. (a) Verse 33—John the Baptist bore witness "to the truth," Jesus; (b) verse 36—the works of Jesus Himself bore witness to who He was; (c) verse 37 so did the Father testify concerning Him; (d) verse 39—the Scriptures themselves bear witness to Jesus; (e) verse 46—Moses, the one the Jews felt they knew the best, also witnessed to Jesus.

18. (a) Jesus rebuked the Pharisees because they rejected the very Scriptures they claimed to know so well. He said to them, "These are the Scriptures that testify about Me, yet you refuse to come to Me to have life" (v. 40). Because they did not accept Jesus, they rejected not only His love, but the Father's as well. (b) Christians must always be careful that they not raise up Bible scholars without raising up people who love God. Many of the people who challenged Jesus were great Bible scholars. But their problem was spelled out clearly by Jesus: "I know that you do not have the love of God in your hearts" (v. 42).

19. The chief priests and teachers of the law during the time of Jesus knew the content of Scripture, but they missed its true meaning and promises. The same can be true for us if our study of the Scriptures does not focus on Jesus as our Savior (v. 39).

Life-Giving Communication

John 6:1–71

Preparing for the Session

Central Focus

After miraculously providing food for five thousand, Jesus offers Himself as a life-giving feast.

Objectives

That participants, by the power of the Holy Spirit working through the Word,

1. count on Jesus to multiply their resources and deal with the crises in their lives;

2. cherish Him, above all, for His life-giving sacrifice;

3. stand by Him faithfully even when others desert Him;

4. seek and accept His pardon for their mistrust, unbelief, and faithlessness.

For the Small-Group Leader

By now your discussion group has made progress in bonding together, and each member feels comfortable sharing personal insights, even shortcomings. Watch out for well-meaning members who may unconsciously monopolize the discussions. If this happens, you may need to end discussion and go on to the next question. Be alert for signals from quiet or shy individuals who indicate they are now ready to share. Provide openings for them and encourage positive reinforcement from the group.

Since this week's lesson contains the account of the feeding of the five thousand, if you feel it appropriate, you might take up an offering to be sent to a world relief agency such as Lutheran World Relief, or some other organization that helps alleviate world hunger. Remind the group that often Jesus works through us to perform His miracles.

Small-Group Discussion Helps

Day 1 • John 6:1–15

1. (a) Philip thought it was impossible to get enough food for so many people: "Eight months' wages would not buy enough bread for each one to have a bite!" (v. 7). (b) Andrew brought a lad who had five barley loaves and two fish but confessed he thought the skinny fish and bread offered little remedy for the situation: "Here is a boy with five small barley loaves and two small fish, but how far will they go among so many?" (v. 9). (c) Matthew records the disciples' solution to the problem: "Send the crowds away, so they can go to the villages and buy themselves some food" (Matthew 14:15).

2. (a) "Have the people sit down" (John 6:10). "Then Jesus directed them to have all the people sit down in groups on the green grass. So they sat down in groups of hundreds and fifties" (Mark 6:39–40). (b) "Jesus then took the loaves, gave thanks" (John 6:10). "He gave thanks" (Mark 6:41). (c) "When they had all had enough to eat" (John 6:12). "They all ate and were satisfied" (Mark 6:42). (d) "He said to His disciples, 'Gather the pieces that are left over. Let nothing be wasted'" (John 6:12). "The disciples picked up twelve basketfuls of broken pieces of bread and fish" (Mark 6:43).

3. Jesus' actions in feeding the large crowd would be a good example for us to follow when we have a problem. He approached the problem in an orderly fashion. He looked to His heavenly Father. He did not waste the resources that the Father abundantly provided. Of course, the solution that Jesus provided was a miracle, something that could only come from the powerful hand of God. But that same power of God is on our side as we attempt to deal with problems in our own lives. Let's responsibly and properly use the resources God gives us and look to His power to make them enough for what we need!

4. Jesus gave thanks for the five barley loaves and two small fish, because He knew what could and would happen to the food. He knew the small amount would

become more than enough for the masses of people. Too often, we, like the disciples, fix our eyes on what is seen and forget about what is unseen (2 Corinthians 4:18). We fail to realize that with Jesus in control, there is always enough!

Day 2 • John 6:16–21

5. In Matthew's account of the same event, we are told Jesus "went up on a mountainside by Himself to pray" (Matthew 14:23). He had just heard the bad news of John's death. His days and nights were filled with people making constant demands. Being human, He got tired, physically and spiritually. He sought to get away, to talk to God. It is a lesson we all need to learn. We need to take time away from life's hustle and bustle to pray, to meditate and talk to God.

6. Many of the words in John 6:16–21 help color the picture of fear for us. "It was dark, and Jesus had not yet joined them" (v. 17). Could anything be more fearful than not to have Jesus present? Fear is highlighted with the description that "a strong wind was blowing and the waters grew rough" (v. 18). The darkness and the wind and the ghostlike appearance of someone coming toward them on the water joined to make them fearful: "They were terrified" (v. 19).

7. The psalmist informs us that God knows everything about us. He knows all our thoughts, all our words, and all our deeds. He knows where we are at all times, and He knows exactly what is happening to us. How comforting and reassuring!

8. Jesus said to them, "It is I; don't be afraid" (v. 20). He assured them of His presence. Nothing is fearful when He is around.

9. The Lord assures us with calming words as well. (a) "So do not fear, for I am with you; do not be dismayed, for I am your God. I will strengthen you and help you; I will uphold you with My righteous right hand" (Isaiah 41:10). (b) "And surely I am with you always, to the very end of the age" (Matthew 28:20). (c) "My grace is sufficient for you, for My power is made perfect in weakness" (2 Corinthians 12:9).

Day 3 • John 6:22–40

10. Jesus told the people, "The work of God is this: to believe in the one He has sent" (v. 29). Believing in Jesus Christ is the "work" God calls for. It is truly a work of God, because believing is always God's doing within us.

11. The words I AM spoken by Jesus amount to much more than the first two words of a simple sentence. When God identified Himself to Moses in calling Moses to lead the Israelites out of Egypt, He named Himself "I AM" (Exodus 3:13–14). Jesus' declarations "I am . . ." pronounced the majestic name of God, a name regarded as so holy by the Jews that they would not say it aloud lest they desecrate it. (a) John 8:12; 9:5—"I am the light of the world." (b) John 10:7, 9—"I am the gate for the sheep." (c) John 10:11, 14 "I am the good shepherd." (d) John 11:25—"I am the resurrection and the life." (e) John 14:6—"I am the way and the truth and the life." (f) John 15:1, 5—"I am the true vine." (g) Encourage participants to share their responses, including an explanation of why they chose the statements they did.

Day 4 • John 6:41–59

12. The Jews accused Jesus of blasphemy. They thought it was ludicrous for Jesus to suggest He was bread "from heaven" (v. 41). After all, they knew who Jesus was. He was only "the son of Joseph, whose father and mother we know" (v. 42).

13. Jesus meets their anger and accusations with the statement, "No one can come to Me unless the Father who sent Me draws him, and I will raise him up at the last day" (v. 44). He was simply saying that people do not draw themselves to the Lord. God draws them!

14. The two kinds of bread from heaven are Jesus, the bread of life, and manna, which the people of Israel ate in the wilderness. Both came as wonderful gifts of God to people who desperately needed them. But, though the manna kept the people in the wilderness alive from day to day, eventually the people died (v. 49). The bread of life gives life forever (vv. 50–51).

15. **Challenge question.** The reference "unless you eat the flesh of the Son of Man and drink His blood, you

have no life in you" (v. 53) refers to faith in Jesus as our Savior from sin and death. Flesh and blood refer to the crucified Christ, the One who died, the One who redeemed us "not with perishable things such as silver or gold . . . but with the precious blood of Christ, a lamb without blemish or defect" (1 Peter 1 :18–19).

Day 5 • John 6:60–71

16. The hard saying that Jesus spoke was of eating His flesh and drinking His blood (v. 56). This was especially repulsive to the Jews, who were forbidden by law to partake of blood.

17. (a) "The Spirit gives life; the flesh counts for nothing. The words I have spoken to you are spirit and they are life" (v. 63). The Spirit uses the Word to give life. Through the Word the Spirit acts and dwells! (b) Let volunteers share their responses. What an assurance to us as we read and study God's Word! The Spirit is using this Word as a tool to strengthen and encourage our faith.

18. They started to desert Jesus because He was headed for trouble. They noted the growing dissension against Jesus. More and more, following Jesus required commitment and sacrifice. It was becoming more and more costly.

19. Impetuous Simon Peter summarizes what is the bottom line for each and every one of us: "Lord, to whom shall we go? You have the words of eternal life. We believe and know that You are the Holy One of God" (vv. 68–69). We have no one else to turn to, in life or in death. He alone has the words of life!

20. Most Bible scholars would agree Judas was not just some pawn who had been set up by Jesus to betray Him. Judas deserted Jesus because he was offered "thirty silver coins" (Matthew 26:15). If Judas, one of the 12 disciples whom Jesus Himself had chosen, could fail the Lord, then certainly we also are not beyond failing Jesus. In fact, Peter earnestly warns us that the devil is out to devour us, too, and that we can only resist him by remaining firm in our faith in Jesus, our only Savior.

21. Encourage participants to share the new insights or renewed convictions they gained from their week's study.

Communication Breakdown

John 7:1–8:30

Preparing for the Session

Central Focus

Despite Jesus' very explicit testimony supported by mighty deeds, those in the best position to accept Him refused Him—a tragic breakdown in communication.

Objectives

That participants, by the power of the Holy Spirit working through the Word,

1. realize that they can and at times do spoil communication from the Lord and His attempts to relate to them;

2. reach out patiently and lovingly to others who are not responding to the Lord's communication with them;

3. point out the forgiveness He offers to those who tune Him out;

4. joyously take advantage of the communication opportunities Jesus provides.

For the Small-Group Leader

As the members of your discussion group get to know one another better, it becomes easier to get bogged down with certain discussion questions, so that you do not complete your entire lesson. As the discussion leader you will need to watch the time and keep moving through the study leaflet. This concern may mean you will have to limit some discussion. If there are times when there are exceptional concerns and needs, you might want to follow up outside the weekly discussion period. Encourage individuals to address some of these concerns also with their pastor.

Small-Group Discussion Helps

Day 1 • John 7:1–24

1. (a) Jesus' brothers wanted the great crowds of people coming to the city for the Feast of Tabernacles to see Jesus' miracles. Their reasoning was that this would help make Him more popular (vv. 3–4). (b) Matthew 13:55–56 mentions four brothers—James, Joseph, Simon, and Judas (Jude)—and sisters as being members of Jesus' family. It also mentions His mother, Mary (indicating that these brothers and sisters were Mary's children and not other relatives). However, Joseph is not mentioned, suggesting that Joseph must have died. Though John tells us that Jesus' brothers did not believe in Him, we later find Jesus' brothers among a gathering of His followers, indicating that they had come to believe in Him, perhaps after His resurrection. In fact, two of Jesus' brothers, James and Jude, became leaders in the church.

2. Among the crowds brought together for the feast there were many opinions about Jesus. Some declared He was a good man; others thought He was nothing more than a deceiver.

3. It is frightening to share the truth about Jesus at times. However, Jesus promises that in the midst of our fear the Holy Spirit will teach us what to say at the right time. This does not mean, of course, that we should not "be prepared to give an answer to everyone who asks you to give a reason for the hope that you have" (1 Peter 3:15). Rather, we are to be certain of the Spirit's guidance and protection.

4. Jesus made it clear that the source of His teaching is God the Father. Jesus did not speak for Himself or for the church or for the rabbis. He spoke for God (v. 16).

5. **Challenge question.** God commanded the people of Israel to keep the Sabbath and to circumcise their sons when they were eight days old. Of these two commands, the command to circumcise took precedence over the command to do no work on the Sabbath. Both commands, however, were meant to cause the Jewish

people to remember God's promise to send the Savior from the seed of Abraham, Isaac, and Jacob (or Israel). Since the meaning of the Sabbath and circumcision were fulfilled in the coming of Jesus the Messiah (or promised Savior), His ministry took precedence over both the Sabbath and circumcision.

6. We misjudge people for the same reason Jesus' opponents misjudged Him: they judged "by mere appearances" (v. 24). We also don't look below the surface, and we fail to appreciate the real beauty deep inside. You might want to lead the class in a prayer at this time, asking forgiveness for those times we have misjudged people.

Day 2 • John 7:25–44

7. Participants will suggest many forms of opposition to Christianity in our world. Even in our part of the world, where a great many people are Christians and church membership constitutes a significant part of the population, our culture is largely secularized. Many religious people see a real attempt by godless people, through media, the judicial system, and education, to rid the civilized world of Christianity as an effective influence on life. The electronic tranquilizer, television, often seems to suggest that every Christian is feebleminded and eccentric. Educators sometimes seem to maintain, "If you can't see it, don't believe it." The religion of secular humanism infiltrates most textbooks. The judicial system often seems to become a law unto itself, ignoring an even wiser, higher law.

8. Jesus said to them, "I go to the one who sent Me . . . but you will not find Me; and where I am, you cannot come" (vv. 33–34). More than likely, they did not know what Jesus was talking about, but, whatever they thought, the statement antagonized them all the more. Some of them may have thought that He would go among the Gentiles and try to lose Himself, so that they would not be able to find Him. If they understood some of His previous statements, that He had been sent by God and that He was headed back to be with God, Jesus' statement must have sounded blasphemous. If they understood what He was really saying, they would also have been insulted to think they could not come to be with the God they claimed to worship.

9. Jesus never stopped proclaiming the good news of

spiritual life available through Him. The Spirit of God would bring about new ways, new possibilities, for those who believe (v. 39).

10. Some said He could not be the Christ, because Christ was to come from Bethlehem, and they thought this man had come from Galilee (vv. 41–42). They were correct in asserting that the Messiah would come from David's line and would be born in Bethlehem, David's hometown. However, they apparently did not know the circumstances of Jesus' birth, that He was descended from David and that He had been born in Bethlehem.

Day 3 • John 7:45–52

11. Nicodemus brought up the issue of justice and legality. He asked, "Does our law condemn anyone without first hearing him to find out what he is doing?" (v. 51). He advocated that Jesus be given a fair hearing before being condemned.

12. (a) The prophet Jonah had come from Galilee (2 Kings 14:25). Gath Hepher was located in the lower part of Galilee, approximately three miles from Nazareth. (b) In Matthew 12:38–41, Jesus even compared Himself to Jonah when He said, "For as Jonah was three days and three nights in the belly of a huge fish, so the Son of Man will be three days and three nights in the heart of the earth."

Day 4 • John 7:53–8:11

13. (a) The Jewish law required death (Leviticus 20:10; Deuteronomy 22:20–24). The Roman law, however, stated that there could be no death sentence without their approval. (b) The Pharisees concluded that either decision on Jesus' part would meet with someone's disapproval.

14. Listen to participants' suggestions. Actually, there is no way of knowing what Jesus wrote in the dust. He may have written something similar to what he said in John 8:7.

15. Note that Jesus offers her forgiveness ("neither do I condemn you") but also admonishes her to sin no more, "Go now and leave your life of sin" (v. 11). In saying this, Jesus clearly declares that sex outside of marriage is a sin, a judgment that Paul by inspiration of God

also clearly maintains in 1 Corinthians 6:18.

16. When under the umbrella of God's forgiving grace, one experiences forgiveness for sins of the past and encouragement and help for the present and future. (a) He assures us of forgiveness for past sins. (b) For present sins He admonishes us to repent and assures us of forgiveness. For the future He warns us to avoid occasions for sin. Jesus joins forgiveness and admonition as He addresses us sinners also.

Day 5 • John 8:12–30

17. *I am* and *light* and *life* are strong assertions and vivid imagery underscoring the deity of Christ.

18. (a) Jesus says clearly that the way to the Father is by knowing Him. He stated in John 14:6: "I am the way and the truth and the life. No one comes to the Father except through Me." (b) Since Jesus is the only way to God, we who know the truth of the Gospel must spread this news as broadly and as quickly as possible so others also may believe the Gospel and be saved. Ministering to the physical needs of people is important. But it is incomplete unless coupled with the message of God's love in Christ.

19. The discussion Jesus had with the Pharisees was important because, as He Himself said, "If you do not believe that I am the one I claim to be, you will indeed die in your sins" (v. 24). His discussion then and now deals with life-and-death matters for them and for us!

20. Jesus was saying that when He was crucified, these people would know He was the Son of God, the promised Messiah.

Communication Breakthrough

John 8:31–9:41

Preparing for the Session

Central Focus

By miraculously restoring sight to a blind man, Jesus prepared him for an even greater miracle—faith—but further alienated His enemies.

Objectives

That participants, by the power of the Holy Spirit working through the Word,

1. joyously take advantage of the communication opportunities Jesus provides;

2. accept their disabilities and limitations as opportunities for God to do something special in their lives;

3. acknowledge that their personal faith is a miracle of spiritual healing and not their own doing;

4. repent of their inclinations to unbelief.

For the Small-Group Leader

As the discussion leader you will want to be especially sensitive when discussing the whole issue of why bad things happen to good people. There may be people in your group who are really hurting over some tragedy in their lives. They may even be angry with God. Try to be understanding of their situation, and yet, at the same time, keep them focused on Christ. There are some things that will only be understood when we know all things—when we're in heaven.

Though physical healing was important to the blind man, Jesus was preparing him for an even greater miracle—faith. All this further alienated Jesus' enemies.

Small-Group Discussion Helps

Day 1 • John 8:31–47

1. "If you hold to My teaching, you are really My disciples," Jesus said (v. 31). We must abide in His Word—in other words, not only hear His words, but also obey His words. Obedience marks discipleship.

2. "Everyone who sins is a slave to sin" (v. 34). While Jesus' opponents imagined that they were free, in actuality they were in bondage to sin so long as they refused to believe in Jesus, who came to set all mankind free from sin. Slaves of sin are set free by the Son. The Son does it through the power of the Word; "The truth will set you free" (v. 32).

3. The devil lied when telling Eve, "You will not surely die." In this temptation, which led to the physical and spiritual death of our first parents and their descendants, we see how the devil is both a liar and a murderer (Genesis 3:1–6). In tempting Jesus, the devil again lied as he twisted God's Word (Matthew 4:1–11). Evil hearts captive to the devil are filled with the hate that leads to murder, as in the case of Cain (1 John 3:12) and all who reject the Father's love in Jesus.

Day 2 • John 8:48–59

4. His opponents respond by calling Jesus "a Samaritan and demon-possessed" (v. 48). Samaritans were outcasts. It was an insult to be called one. Jesus replied in three different ways: (a) Verse 49—"I am not possessed by a demon, but I honor My Father and you dishonor Me"; (b) Verse 50—"I am not seeking glory for Myself; but there is one who seeks it, and He is the judge." In other passages (John 5:22; 2 Corinthians 5:10), Jesus Himself is identified as the One who will judge at the Last Day. This is because the Father, who is the Judge of all, has appointed Christ to judge on His behalf (Acts 10:42; 17:31; Romans 2:16). (c) Verse 51—"I tell you the truth, if anyone keeps My word, he will never see death."

5. They concluded Jesus was really demon-possessed

after hearing His claim to be able even to avoid death. They couldn't believe that He claimed something that wasn't true for Abraham and the other famous prophets—the claim that He could prevent death.

6. Once again Jesus echoed the words of Exodus 3:14. Abraham died, but even before Abraham, Jesus proclaimed, "I am." Jesus existed before Abraham lived or died.

7. Answers will vary. Encourage the participants to share which claim(s) of Jesus is (are) most meaningful and why.

....

Day 3 • John 9:1–12

8. (a) Sometimes a specific sin has a direct consequence, illness and even death. Let participants suggest modern-day examples, such as sexual promiscuity leading to a sexually transmitted disease. (b) God intended not only that this man should come to faith and receive eternal life, but that through him and this event others might be led to faith and life.

9. (a) Philippians 1:12, 29—God tells us He sometimes allows suffering for the advancement of the Gospel. Because Paul was willing to suffer for the Gospel, others were able to hear it. (b) 2 Corinthians 1:35—suffering might be allowed so that we might be better equipped to understand (empathize with) someone else who is suffering. (For example, someone who has gone through depression might better understand and counsel someone else going through depression.) (c) Hebrews 12:5–11—He sometimes allows suffering to discipline His people. (d) James 1:2–4—At times, suffering takes place to produce spiritual growth in God's chosen people.

10. Isaiah and other prophets foretold that when the Messiah came, He would, among other deeds, give sight to the blind. Jesus' healing the blind was a sign that in Jesus God had fulfilled His promises to send the Messiah. That was part of the message that Jesus sent back to John the Baptist through John's disciples.

11. We must always keep in mind the truth recorded by James: "Now listen, you who say, 'Today or tomorrow we will go to this or that city, spend a year there, carry on business and make money.' Why, you do not even know what will happen tomorrow. What is your life?

You are a mist that appears for a little while and then vanishes. Instead, you ought to say, 'If it is the Lord's will, we will live and do this or that.' As it is, you boast and brag. All such boasting is evil. Anyone, then, who knows the good he ought to do and doesn't do it, sins" (James 4:13–17).

12. Jesus came to overcome the darkness of (a) sin, or evil, (b) death, (c) the power of the devil.

13. Answers here will and may vary. The blind man responded to Jesus' command to "Go, wash in the Pool of Siloam," so like the lepers (Luke 17:14) the beginning of faith was probably stirring in his heart. (Complete faith came later; John 9:38.) No doubt hope and expectation battled with doubt as he went to carry out Jesus' command.

....

Day 4 • John 9:13–34

14. Encourage participants to share their answers.

15. Answers will vary. Perhaps many would say that they would have been much more willing to testify as to what had happened; however, in those days there was a great deal of shame and humiliation connected with being cast out of the synagogue.

16. **Challenge question.** The Pharisees were asking the man to tell the truth when they said, "Give glory to God" (v. 24). But their motive, of course, was not to glorify God but to discredit Jesus. A similar request (not made hypocritically) is made by Joshua of Achan, "My son, give glory to the Lord" (Joshua 7:19).

17. (a) He knew he had been blind and now could see as a result of what Jesus had done. (b) We also may not know everything about Jesus—perhaps not nearly as much as others do. But we can testify about what we do know, that through Him we have forgiveness of our sins, peace with God, and many blessings. Some participants in your group may be keenly aware of the limitations to their spiritual or Bible knowledge. Encourage them that no one has to know all the answers (who of us does?) to lead someone to Jesus, the Savior.

18. The once-blind man concluded that Jesus was able to make him see (v. 25). As they continued to inquire about Jesus, the blind man, a little irritated by it all, simply challenged them by asking, "Do you want to become His disciples, too?" (v. 27). Obviously, many

people were following Jesus. After additional insults, the man simply reminded them that unless Jesus had been from God He would not have been able to perform this marvelous miracle.

19. The Pharisees regarded the formerly blind man as "steeped in sin at birth" because he had been born blind, which they believed was the result of sin either sin committed by the man's parents, so that God gave them a blind son, or sin that he himself had committed before he was born. Prejudices (which literally are conclusions drawn before you know the facts) are common in our own thinking too. One way we let prejudices form is by over generalizing. On the basis of one experience, we say, "All the people in this category are like that." This is sinful judging. What we think we know isn't always so. And people can be hurt by the prejudices we form. We ought to be careful about drawing conclusions about people, especially when we have no first-hand knowledge of the truth.

. . . .

Day 5 • John 9:35–41

20. "He found Him" (v. 35). Jesus, whose heart is filled with compassion and seeking love for those who are lost, reaches out to find the lost ones. He came to seek and save the lost.

21. Now that He has set the groundwork, Jesus is direct. He asks, "Do you believe in the Son of Man?" (v. 35). The man asked, "Who is He, sir?" (v. 36). Jesus responded immediately, identifying Himself as the Son of Man. We must also be willing and bold enough to ask the question, "Do you believe in the Son of Man, Jesus Christ?" And we must be willing to give witness to who Jesus really is, the Savior of the world, the One who came so that the world might not perish (John 3:16).

22. (a) Belief brought about worship! Already grateful for what Jesus had done for him, the man now realizes that he is in the presence of his God, who has cared for him all his life. No doubt he was also aware of God's promises to send the Messiah (the Savior). Realizing that he has now seen the Messiah, the man worships. (b) Our belief does the same thing. We are led to worship the One we believe in, Jesus Christ. He is our Creator and Redeemer. We owe so much to Him. He deserves our worship.

23. (a) Admission of one's spiritual blindness is necessary before one can be cured. The Pharisees insisted that they could see, and because of their stubbornness, they remained in their sin. (b) Many sins, such as pride, anger, an unforgiving spirit, might be keeping us from 20/20 spiritual vision. Do not ask anyone to share, but be ready to listen to and support, with your love and the message of the Gospel, anyone who wants to speak in response to the question. (c) The steps we must take are to search our hearts honestly, to confess our sins, and to receive God's forgiveness. Then we will see ourselves as we are and see God as He is.

Communication at Its Best

John 10:1–42

Preparing for the Session

Central Focus

Jesus describes the close, caring, saving relationship He has with those who hear and accept Him.

Objectives

That participants, by the power of the Holy Spirit working through the Word,

1. recognize as true spiritual leaders only those who lead others to God and His people through Jesus;

2. listen eagerly to the voice of Jesus in Word and Sacrament;

3. experience closeness and security in their relationship to Him as their God and Savior.

For the Small-Group Leader

Today you are discussing one of the most comforting chapters in all of John's Gospel. Jesus calls Himself the Good Shepherd (John 10:11). As the discussion leader, show excitement in knowing that this Good Shepherd knows each person by name and that He loves each member of the group so much that He gave His life for each one of them.

Small-Group Discussion Helps

Day 1 • John 10:1–6

1. Psalm 23 pictures the shepherd as vital for the well-being of the sheep. The shepherd provides in every way for the care of the sheep. Instinctively the sheep know the shepherd has made plans for their care; "The Lord is my shepherd, I shall not want" (Psalm 23:1 KJV). The same thought is found in Isaiah 40:11 and Ezekiel 34:11–16. The common attitude throughout is the overwhelming care of the shepherd for his sheep.

2. Jesus here speaks of false prophets or religious leaders then and now—people who, like the Pharisees and the teachers of the law, deceive people about the way to salvation. They can be identified as false prophets because they do not enter "by the gate"—that is, they do not point to Jesus and Him alone as the only gate to heaven.

3. How comforting to know that, with the billions of people in the world, He knows each of us by name!

4. We hear the voice of Jesus in the words of Scripture, particularly as they testify of His forgiving love. Listening to His voice means to believe in Him, to take to heart what He says to us in all the words of the Bible, and to grow to become like Him as we obediently do what He tells us to do.

5. The Pharisees did not understand what Jesus was telling them because they hardened their hearts to His words. They rejected Jesus and thus simply could not understand the truth hidden in this parable of the shepherd and sheep.

Day 2 • John 10:7–10

6. Jesus Christ is the only entrance to the sheepfold (vv. 7, 9).

7. Because they do not place their belief in Jesus Christ as Lord and Savior, religions and sects that teach another way to salvation come "only to steal and kill and destroy" (v. 10).

8. (a) John 14:6 reminds us that there is only one way to God. It is through Jesus Christ who is "the way and the truth and the life." (b) In Acts 4:12 we are told "salvation is found in one else, for there is no other name under heaven given to men by which we must be saved." (c) 1 Timothy 2:5 states that "there is one God and one mediator between God and men, the man Christ Jesus."

9. The interest of the thief is "to steal and kill and destroy." The shepherd's intent is to come "that they may have life, and have it to the full" (v. 10).

10. Jesus desires the best for all people. But we do not always know what that best is. God knows that the best is in the world to come, not in this world, and He does not want anything in this life to distract us from our heavenly goal. In fact, even now He uses our suffering to shape us into people who are growing to be more like Christ. So, even when our circumstances seem to be less than the best in this world, we Christians can have joy deep down in our hearts because we are confident that nothing can separate us from God and His love. While we may have to be patient for a time, soon we will enter into the joy of our Lord. The indescribably wonderful future God has in mind for us is indeed life in all its fullness, as we are even now being "transformed into His likeness" (2 Corinthians 3:18). And one day we "shall be like Him, for we shall see Him as He is" (1 John 3:2).

Day 3 • John 10:11–16

11. (a) A good shepherd is willing to "lay down His life for the sheep" (John 10:11). David reminded Saul of the same truth in 1 Samuel 17:34–37. (b) He redeemed us (bought us back) from the curse of the Law, the condemnation of eternal death we deserve because we have not kept God's Law. His resurrection guarantees that we also shall rise from the dead and live eternally with Him.

12. He gives His life for the sheep, because, unlike the hired hand who "cares nothing for the sheep," Jesus loves the sheep and cares for them (v. 13).

13. There is a deep intimacy between the Good Shepherd and the sheep as indicated by the fact the Good Shepherd knows His sheep personally and His sheep know Him, "just as the Father knows [the Good Shepherd] and [the Good Shepherd] know[s] the Father" (v. 15).

14. (a) The other sheep referred to are the nations outside of Judaism, particularly the Gentiles—all non-Jews. Thus, all people are included in Jesus' work of redemption. He wants everyone to be part of His flock. (b) Jesus sends us to bring the other sheep into the sheep pen. Just as Peter and Paul took the Gospel to the Gentiles, so we are to take the Good News to all people. It is to be done locally as well as to foreign countries through missionaries we help support.

15. We can be sure we listen to Jesus' voice, even though surrounded by so many other voices calling for our attention, by searching the Word of God and by judging everything we hear in the light of what God tells us.

Day 4 • John 10:17–21

16. Jesus makes it clear that His final act of laying down His life for His sheep is an act prompted by obedience to His Father and love for His sheep (vv. 17–18). He also claims that no one takes His life, but that He lays it down voluntarily. He further claims that He will take it up again by His resurrection.

17. Jesus willingly laid down His life (John 10:18). Because He did this by His own choice and would then rise in triumph over death and the devil, Jesus' death did not show weakness. Rather, it revealed His strength and power as God's Son.

18. This meditation was suggested for home use. Move to the next question unless someone wants to share what the text and her or his meditation meant personally.

19. These strong affirmations—His claims of voluntarily laying down His life and being able to raise it up again—brought division among the Jewish leaders (v. 19). Some of the Jews concluded that only a demon-possessed man would make such claims. Others, however, were confused, because they knew Jesus had healed a blind man, and certainly a demon could not "open the eyes of the blind" (v. 21). Again, the division was based on unbelief contending with belief.

Day 5 • John 10:22–42

20. In John 8:56–58 Jesus made it clear that He was God. He was with Abraham, the one they claimed was their father, but more than that He said, "I AM," meaning He always was, because He was God. Indeed, He had answered the question of whether or not He was the Christ long before, but, because of their unbelief, they did not hear what He had told them.

21. (a) Verse 27—"I know them, and they follow Me." (b) Verse 28—"I give them eternal life, and they shall never perish; no one can snatch them out of My hand."

22. (a) Answers will vary. (b) He further promises that

no one can snatch a Christian out of the Father's hand, since God's power to preserve us is greater than the power of the devil or any other opponent to take us away from Him (vv. 28b, 29b). (c) This promise is an important reassurance to us when we consider the great power and slyness of the devil and our own weakness. Though we would soon fall before the devil's attack, God will protect and preserve us. (d) Though no power can pry us out of God's care and keeping, we ourselves may fall away from God by our own choice. The idea that no Christian can fall away from God is not scriptural. Jesus speaks about believers who believe for a time and then fall away in the parable of the sower (Matthew 13:20–22), and Paul refers to Jews who were among God's people but who were cut off because they would not accept Jesus as the Messiah. He affirms, however, that God could graft them in once again if they would stop their persistent unbelief and receive Jesus as the Messiah (Romans 11:22–23). (Scripture also teaches that Christians can fall away in Hebrews 6:4–6.)

23. They thought Jesus had committed blasphemy by stating "I and the Father are one" (v. 30). The penalty for blasphemy was stoning (Leviticus 24:16).

24. **Challenge question.** (a) Jesus reasoned that if unrighteous judges were called "gods" because they were privileged with speaking the Word of God (Psalm 82:6), it seemed only right that the "one whom the Father set apart as His very own and sent into the world" (v. 36) should not be stoned to death for calling Himself God. (b) In quoting Psalm 82, Jesus points out that the Scripture cannot be broken (must always be right).

25. The reception is different because John the Baptist had prepared the people through repentance and Baptism.

26. Encourage the participants to share with the class blessings they have personally received from the Good Shepherd. Certainly, at the top of most lists would be forgiveness of sins. You might even want to list the blessings on a chalkboard and then offer a prayer, thanking God for these many blessings.

Ultimate Purpose: Death-Transcending Relationships

John 11:1–57

Preparing for the Session

Central Focus

By raising His dead friend to life, Jesus points to what He will accomplish through His own death and resurrection—a relationship with His followers that extends beyond death.

Objectives

That participants, by the power of the Holy Spirit working through the Word,

1. bring their needs to Jesus;

2. face death with the sure hope of life eternal through Jesus' death and resurrection;

3. find comfort in the fact that their relationships with Him and believing loved ones will never end;

4. accept delay as a sign of His love;

5. recognize the death and resurrection of Lazarus as a prelude to Jesus' death and resurrection and all that they will accomplish.

For the Small-Group Leader

As discussion leader you have put in many extra hours in helping others grow in their walk with the Lord; however, as you have given of your time and talent, so you have been blessed in immeasurable ways. Thank you for a job well done! Jesus says to you, "Well done, good and faithful servant" (Matthew 25:23).

Remind your group that your study and time together do not have to end with this session. The second study of John will begin soon and the participants will want to begin a new LifeLight adventure. Share with them that this week's lesson, the raising of Lazarus, is only a prelude to greater things to come, the raising up of believers for a wonderful eternity through Christ's own death and resurrection. The best is yet to come, as they will discover in the next study. Encourage the members to invite a friend to join in this adventure.

Conclude your session this week with a prayer, thanking God for all that you have learned together, for your ministry to each other during this study, and for God's continued blessings on the next LifeLight study.

Small-Group Discussion Helps

Day 1 • John 11:1–16

1. Don't spend a lot of time on this. Its purpose is to provide a quick review and introduction to the narrative. One volunteer for each of the five Bible persons may simply read what he or she has jotted down. Then move on.

The persons mentioned are (a) Jesus, (b) Lazarus, (c) Mary, (d) Martha, and (e) Thomas. Jesus had been befriended by the family of Lazarus, Mary, and Martha. Mary and Martha had opened up their home at different times to Jesus.

Lazarus was the brother of Mary and Martha. He and his sisters were from Bethany. After Jesus had resurrected Lazarus, many people came to see him, obviously not quite believing that it had happened as they had heard. When some of the chief priests saw Lazarus, a few of them even suggested Lazarus be put back to death (John 12:10).

Martha was a sister of Lazarus and Mary. When we think of Martha, we often think of the story recorded in Luke 10:38–42 where Martha was in the kitchen preparing food for Jesus, while Mary sat at His feet listening to His words. Martha became annoyed and asked Jesus to have Mary help her. Jesus responded with the words, "Martha, Martha, you are worried and upset about many things, but only one thing is needed. Mary has chosen what is better, and it will not be taken away from her" (Luke 10:41–42). Martha obviously liked cooking because, once again, in John 12:1–10, when a dinner was given for Jesus and His disciples after Lazarus's resurrection, she was involved with serving.

Mary was more meditative. She sat at Jesus' feet listening to His every word (Luke 10:39). At the special celebration dinner served after Lazarus's resurrection, Mary showed her appreciation and joy by anointing Jesus' feet with costly perfume (John 12:1–9).

Thomas, mentioned in verse 16, is the disciple who remained disbelieving longer than the others after Jesus had risen from the dead. Permit participants simply to say what they know about these persons.

2. Lazarus is introduced as "the one You [Jesus] love" (v. 3). The entire family, which included Lazarus, Mary, and Martha, were very close to Jesus as indicated by Jesus' frequent visits to their home.

3. (a) Lazarus had gotten sick and died to bring God glory, "so that God's Son may be glorified through it" (v. 4). (b) By raising Lazarus from the dead, Jesus would do His greatest and final miraculous sign before His crucifixion and resurrection. As He thus revealed Himself as the Son of God and the divine Savior, the purpose was to bring people to faith in Him. As John 11:14 and 45 indicate, this purpose was achieved in the strengthening of the disciples' faith and in the many who "put their faith in Him" as a result of this miracle.

4. They were beginning to recognize that Jesus was going to be put to death. It was inevitable. Thomas even suggested that they all go to "die with Him" (v. 16).

5. (a) Most all of us have experienced the death of someone close and important to us and the resulting grief. (b) In verse 11 Jesus reminds us that He will wake up the dead, those who have "fallen asleep." The term *sleep* emphasizes that death is not permanent but is a temporary state from which the sleeper wakens. Jesus here gives a hint that He will raise Lazarus from the dead even as, at the Last Day, He will raise all of us from the dead (John 5:28–29). (c) Immediately upon death the soul enters the joy of heaven.

Day 2 • John 11:17–37

6. The widow of Nain's son was raised in the course of his funeral, normally conducted the day after death. The daughter of Jairus had just died.

7. (a) Martha rushed out to meet Jesus and expressed great faith. She recognized that had Jesus been there, her brother would not have died. She was also convinced

that if He wanted something and asked His Father for it, it would be granted. After Jesus said Lazarus would be resurrected, Martha answered, "I know he will rise again in the resurrection at the last day" (v. 24). Again, she expressed great faith in her confession found in verse 27, "Yes, Lord, I believe that You are the Christ, the Son of God, who was to come into the world." Verse 22 may indicate that she did not fully realize that He is God, equal with the Father. (b) Mary expressed the same belief as Martha in that she says, "Lord, if You had been here, my brother would not have died" (v. 32).

8. It was part of Jesus' human nature to weep just as we do at times. How comforting to know that Jesus felt what we do, that Jesus can sympathize with us (Hebrews 4:15). He Himself as a true human being knows from experience our griefs, sufferings, and trials.

9. We have many promises God speaks to us in our sorrows. (a) Psalm 46:1 reminds us that "God is our refuge and strength" in every trouble. (b) Psalm 55:22 promises, "Cast your cares on the Lord and He will sustain you." For whatever reason we cry, Jesus will help us. (c) In 1 Thessalonians 4:13–14 we are told that we do not have to "grieve like the rest of men, who have no hope," because "we believe that Jesus died and rose again and so we believe that God will bring with Jesus those who have fallen asleep in Him."

10. **Challenge question.** People go through different stages of grief whenever there is a major loss, such as death or loss of job. Mary and Martha must have gone through some of these stages of grief as well. Lazarus's sisters must have experienced shock. Lazarus may well have been a young man when he died, perhaps no older than Jesus (about 30). "Many Jews had come to Martha and Mary to comfort them in the loss of their brother" (v. 19). Emotional release is healthy when a loved one dies, as indicated by Jesus' own crying (v. 35). We can assume that Mary and Martha also wept over their great loss. Depression or loneliness follows the death of a loved one. During this stage we ask questions such as, "What will I do without him?" or "Why didn't God answer my prayers for her recovery?" Even men like David cried out in isolation at times (Psalm 42:5). Both Martha and Mary had to have felt a little let down that Jesus didn't arrive in time to heal Lazarus and may have even laid some blame on Him (John 11:21, 32). Panic accompanies fear. Mary and Martha may have felt panic

because their means of support, with Lazarus, may have been taken from them. Guilt over things said or not said often plagues someone who mourns the death of a loved one, or guilt about what he or she might have done to prevent the death. (For example, a wife may feel guilty because she didn't rush her husband to the hospital soon enough after he started having chest pains.) Mary and Martha may have felt hostility or resentment toward God because He allowed Lazarus to die. We often look for someone to blame.

Day 3 • John 11:38–41

11. The stone is removed as evidence that Lazarus was really in the tomb and actually dead. The odor, if not the sight, must have accentuated the fact.

12. Martha, like many of us, may have fluctuated in her faith. She knew Jesus could raise Lazarus to life (v. 22) and would definitely raise everyone on the Last Day (v. 24), but she wasn't quite sure about whether or not He could do it right then, especially since Lazarus had been dead for four days (v. 39). Of course, such thoughts would not have been consistent with the faith that Martha had expressed, but who of us is consistent in our faith?

13. In part, Jesus' gift of life to Lazarus led to His own death; however, the raising of Lazarus was a foretaste of an even greater resurrection that would take place, the resurrection of those who believed through the life, death, and resurrection of Jesus Christ.

Day 4 • John 11:45–57

14. The bottom line was unadulterated jealousy. "If we let Him go on like this, everyone will believe in Him, and then the Romans will come and take away both our place and our nation" (v. 48). Mixed in with their jealousy was fear that Rome might be led to unleash its great power and destroy them all.

15. (a) Caiaphas clearly was thinking only of political survival when he determined that Jesus needed to die for the good of the people. (b) But the high priest's words were truer than even he expected. The death of Jesus would save the nation from destruction—a spiritual destruction.

16. He withdrew because the exact time for Him to die had not yet come. Jesus and the Father—not Jesus' opponents—remained in control of the events leading to His crucifixion.

17. (a) Jesus knew He was going to die. His prayer in the Garden of Gethsemane reveals to us the dread He felt about this approaching ordeal. Yet He also faced this prospect with joy, because by it He would accomplish His mission and save the world from sin and death. (b) Knowing how Jesus felt can become our comfort and assurance, because we know we have someone who can "sympathize with our weaknesses" (Hebrews 4:15).

Day 5

18. As each member of the class studied the Word, each one had the opportunity to come to believe more fully "that Jesus is the Christ, the Son of God, and that by believing you may have life in His name" (John 20:31).

19. Answers will vary. Share with the other participants some of the verses that have become your favorites through this LifeLight study and explain why.

20. Use this question to encourage everyone to enroll in the next LifeLight study of the second half of John. Suggest that each person bring at least one new person into the program.

Close your time together with prayers of thanks and joy for the blessings your group has received. Assure one another of continued prayers, support, and love.

The Messenger Is the Message

1. The prologue is the key that unlocks the Gospel of John.

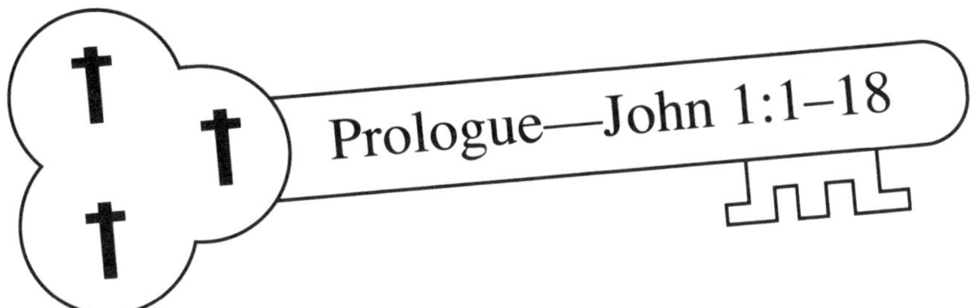

We are introduced to Jesus—the main character in this amazing story.

There is much more to Him than you might think.

There never was and never will be anyone just like Him!

2. The author is Jesus' best friend.

Who can better help us to know Jesus than His closest human friend?

John was a fisherman; he was boisterous, extroverted, and ambitious.

Learn about Jesus from one who was there when it all happened.

John saw Him with his own eyes, heard Him with his own ears, experienced Him from within a close personal relationship.

The Messenger Is the Message

3. Jesus uses simple terms with deep meaning.

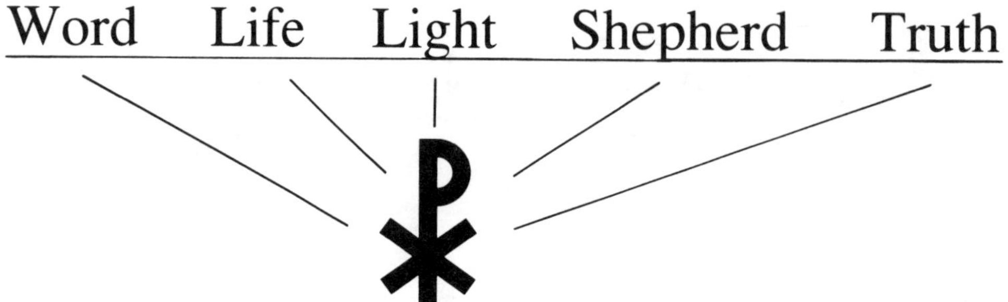

Short, common, easy-to-understand words:

Word	Bread	Shepherd
Life	Water	Truth
Light	Sheep	Way

These words open up the secrets of God's heart.

They reveal mysteries of the universe.

They need to be carefully defined and clearly understood.

When we dig down deep enough into these terms, we discover that they point to *Jesus.*

The Messenger Is the Message

4. The messenger is the message and the sender!

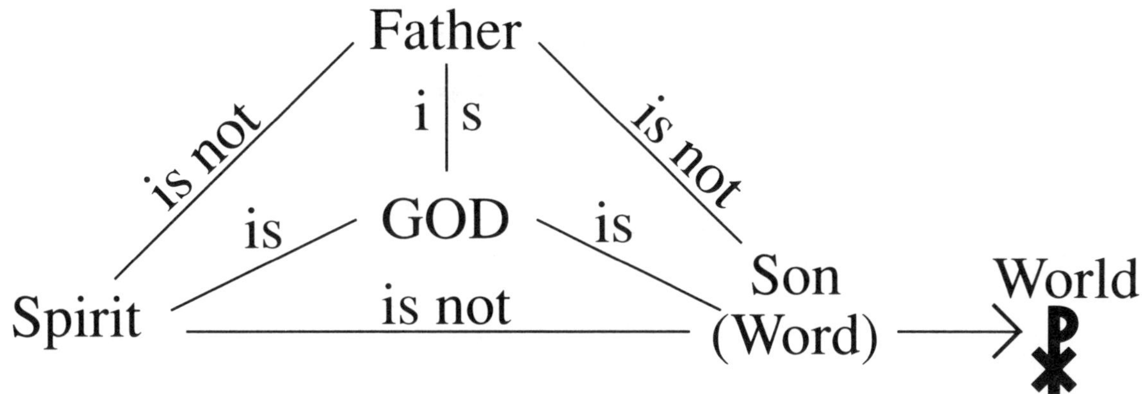

Ours is a triune God—one God in three distinct persons.

(Father is not the Son, Son is not the Spirit, etc. But all three are true God.)

One of these divine persons—the Son (Word)—came into the world.

The Messenger Is the Message

5. God communicates by becoming one of us.

   He is so vast, holy, and complicated; we cannot understand Him or feel close to Him.

   So that we can get to know and love Him and communicate with Him, His Son became a true human being, just like us, except not sinful.

   Although truly human, Jesus was also true God.

   To know about God, to know God personally, become better acquainted with the man Jesus.

   He is God in human flesh and form, communicating with us in human terms as one of us.

6. Jesus' communication both reveals and conceals.

   While among us, God's Son faced life in the same terms that we do.

   He used His divine power only to make God's love and power known by helping others—never for helping Himself.

   The sinful heart of humans rejects a God who humbles Himself as a human being. Yet those who in faith receive Him by the power of God's Spirit become nothing less than God's own children.

   He is the light of God, the glory of God—presence and power of God in visible form.

   To open our eyes to Him (believe) requires a miracle, but we can close our eyes in unbelief all by ourselves.

The Messenger Is the Message

7. The heart of the message: God loves us.

God loves us more than we ever imagined, even though we don't deserve this (grace!).

In Jesus He kept His promises to help us (truth!).

In love He deals with our sinfulness, although this was not easy to do.

The Messenger Is the Message

8. The purpose of God's communication is a close personal relationship.

Warm personal communication builds close personal relationships. That's why God sent Jesus.

He builds a parent-child relationship between us and God.

He connects us closely to God in saving faith (life!).

Expect this relationship to grow stronger as we study the Gospel of John.